Leading Learning That Matters

A Leadership Process to Rethink What's Taught and How for Today's World

Leading Learning that Matters

Flossie S. G. Chua
David N. Perkins and
Daniel G. Wilson

Copyright © 2021 by Flossie S. G. Chua, David N. Perkins, and Daniel G. Wilson

Leading Learning that Matters: A Leadership Process to Rethink What's Taught and How for Today's World was produced by F. Chua, D. Perkins, and D. Wilson, researchers at Project Zero, a research center at the Harvard Graduate School of Education in Cambridge, MA, USA, based on work done with Independent Schools Victoria, VIC, Australia.

This copyrighted work is licensed under the Creative Commons Attribution-NonCommercial-NoDerivatives 4.0 International License (CC BY-NC-ND). This allows users to share this work with others if they credit F. Chua, D. Perkins, & D. Wilson of Project Zero, a research center at the Harvard Graduate School of Education in Cambridge, MA, USA, working with Independent Schools Victoria, VIC, Australia. This work cannot be changed in any way or used commercially.

The Tools and Tips in Part III of the book are licensed under the Creative Commons Attribution-NonCommercial 4.0 International License (CC BY-NC 4.0). Users are free to share and adapt these tools if users credit F. Chua, D. Perkins, & D. Wilson of Project Zero, a research center at the Harvard Graduate School of Education in Cambridge, MA, USA, working with Independent Schools Victoria, VIC, Australia. If any modifications are made to the tools, users must indicate this without suggesting that F. Chua, D. Perkins, and D. Wilson have endorsed the modifications.

ISBN: 978-0-578-84635-4

Book design by Alex Camlin

Acknowledgments

Leading Learning that Matters (LLtM) is a research collaboration between Project Zero (PZ), a research center at the Harvard Graduate School of Education, and Independent Schools Victoria (ISV), an association of more than 220 independent schools in Victoria, Australia, which conducts a wide range of activities enhancing school leadership and teaching practices. The goal of LLtM is to develop a framework and process to help schools flexibly rethink aspects of what they teach, how, and why, toward education that speaks powerfully to life in today's complex world.

The LLtM initiative is funded by Independent Schools Victoria and its participating member schools, guided by the vision and inspiration of ISV Chief Executive Michelle Green, whom we deeply thank for her insight, collaboration, and support. We also greatly appreciate our very generative relationship with Kate Anderson, Michele Bernshaw, and Aynur Simsirel of ISV, who have contributed to the evolving LLtM model and to its day-to-day coordination; and Karin Morrison, who contributed during the early years of envisioning and launching LLtM.

We are immensely grateful to all three cohorts of LLtM principals who trusted in the LLtM process and shared their experiences with our team. Without their input and support, we would not have been able to conceptualize, test, and refine the LLtM framework and tools.

The first cohort of principals participated in the initial research and development phase of LLtM, experimenting energetically, sharing insights, and supporting one another as critical friends.

The second cohort of LLtM principals was deeply thoughtful about what it meant to encourage learners for a complex world and courageous in their willingness to explore what leading such work looked like in their own contexts.

The third cohort of principals pushed our thinking further as they experimented with the LLtM framework and process and offered astute and perceptive feedback toward refining the tools featured in this book.

We look forward to future cohorts of principals whose participation in the LLtM program will continue to help us rethink and refine the LLtM framework and process, even as we encourage school leaders anywhere in the world to engage the ideas and tools offered here in ways that seem productive to them.

Last but not least, we thank several people who have contributed to the production of this book in important ways. PZ researcher Carin Aquiline was outstanding in her editorial work on the book—attentive to the overall framing, meticulous with the details, and collaborative on all aspects. Shane Green of ISV was hugely generous in providing detailed and valuable feedback, with recommendations instrumental in improving the text.

Alex Camlin's artistic book design took our initial ideas to a professional level that we had not thought possible; his guidance on layouts and graphics to illuminate the message was striking. Jane Ellin was precise and careful in her copyediting, with an acute sense of how one communicates compellingly through words.

At various junctures, several other individuals at ISV and PZ offered insightful feedback on content, titling, design, and other matters, improving the book in numerous ways. We appreciate the generosity and commitment of them all!

The Roles of the Authors

Broadly speaking, *Leading Learning that Matters* was a thoroughly collaborative undertaking. All three authors interacted extensively with the participating principals as well as sharing in the construction and refinement of the LLtM framework and the writing.

Flossie Chua took particular responsibility for conducting interviews, documenting practices, and crafting the pictures of practice in the first section, as well as serving as principal editor of this book in its entirety. Many of the concepts about learning that matters and the tools mentioned here and detailed in Part III were adapted from *Future Wise: Educating Our Children for a Changing World* by David Perkins. Daniel Wilson, drawing on his knowledge of and research into leadership and collaborative processes, played the principal role in constructing and refining the leadership framework.

Brief biographies of the authors appear at the end of this volume.

Table of Contents

Introduction ix

Part I. Pictures of Practice

Fostering Personal Significance and Passion in Learning 3
Learning about Migration, Developing Multiple Perspective-Taking & Empathy 9
Exploring Literature as a Lens on the World and the Self 17
Developing Reflective Capacity and Resilience through Self-Managed Learning 25
Building Bridges Between Important Content and Personal Meaning 33

Part II. Navigating the Journey

Visions of the Learning that Matters 39
Four Leadership Practices 47
The First Months 53
On the Journey Together 61

Part III. Tools and Tips

Building and Refining Visions for Learning that Matters 67
    Beyonding Education 71
    Mattermatics 73
    Expanding Topics to Matter More 75
    Opportunity Story 79
    Accept No Substitutes 81
Leading Learning that Matters 83
    Documenting Learning that Matters 87
    Ecology of Social Influences 89
    Learning Frame and Windows 91
    Voices to Vision 93
    Ladder of Feedback 95
    Edge Effect 97
    Key Change Roles 99

About the Authors 100

Introduction

Education is a more exciting—and more tumultuous—undertaking today than it has been in decades. While high-stakes testing is an important wide-scale practice, it's also generally recognized that what's actually tested does not always align with what we most want students to learn. While in-person learning remains the desirable default, online methods serving circumstances of necessity or convenience introduce new rhythms of learning that can inspire new visions for what might be learned. Around the world, in national standards and within individual schools and coalitions of schools, not only *how* we teach but *what* we teach has become a front of exploration.

In some settings, 21st century skills—including skills of critical and creative thinking, collaboration, citizenship, entrepreneurship, and more—are receiving serious attention. In some, shifting beyond local or national concerns to encourage global perspectives is playing a more central role. And in other schools, personalized learning attuned to the particular passions of individual students plays a central role—not at the expense of fundamentals like literacy, numeracy, and basic knowledge, but woven artfully into and among those fundamentals to energize the learning process.

These trends are not universal. But they are strong and notable. Why?

Thoughtful educators are recognizing that educating for today's and tomorrow's world is a very different proposition from educating for the latter half of the 20th century. Globalization introduces both opportunities for and challenges to what it means to participate politically and economically. Global issues such as climate change and energy supplies are becoming critical. High population mobility means that many people are likely to live and work and participate as citizens in settings distant from their places of birth, not uncommonly in different nations altogether. The gradual shift around the world from a manufacturing society to an information society, from production to services, is changing the character of work and what it means to be prepared for that work.

In this volatile and exciting context, many educators are becoming increasingly engaged by one of education's fundamental questions: *What kind of learning really matters?* That is, *What agile skills and expansive understandings best prepare today's learners to thrive in our complex world? How can our school innovate in smaller or larger ways to position itself as a strong and distinctive contributor to our students' lives in this complex world?*

Leading Learning that Matters

Such questions can be approached on many levels. Leading Learning that Matters is a flexibly structured process for individual schools and small coalitions of schools that invites participating school leaders and their faculties and communities to engage in a reflective process of rethinking some aspects of what's taught and how it's taught. It encourages participants to construct a vision and to make that vision a daily reality in courses and classrooms throughout the institution.

Does this sound like a tall order? It is! But it is not out of reach. Here's why . . .

Leading Learning that Matters (let's call it LLtM for short) has no fixed answer to what learning matters. Schools are encouraged to construct their own visions, reflecting their history, their ongoing commitments, and their sense of the world for which they are preparing students.

LLtM takes it for granted that any school already is doing a great deal toward *learning that matters*. The goal is to honor and make the most of what's already there and extend it.

LLtM has great respect for educational fundamentals that have universal importance, such as strong literacy and mathematics skills.

LLtM recognizes the importance of a collaborative community process within and beyond the school, and often across coalitions of schools. What a declaration from higher up can rarely do, a genuinely collaborative community process generally can.

LLtM provides helpful pictures of practice illustrating what prior participants have done; general guidelines for the process; and a toolkit of key questions to ask, checklists to bear in mind, diagrams that help organize, and more.

Finally, LLtM recognizes that any manageable and productive quest in that spirit will not unfold overnight. Generous time, always with the proviso that things keep moving forward, is core to the endeavor.

The origins of Leading Learning that Matters

LLtM emerged from a collaboration between Project Zero, a research center at the Harvard Graduate School of Education with fifty-plus years of educational innovations, and Independent Schools Victoria, an association of more than 220 independent schools in Victoria, Australia.

Independent Schools Victoria sponsored a pilot initiative involving eleven schools. Early versions of the framework guided the schools' explorations of LLtM. Much of the framework emerged from the reflections and experiences of the principals and other leader figures and teachers in the schools.

These efforts are continuing.

How schools decide to engage Leading Learning that Matters

Perhaps the basic answer to how schools decide is this: they don't decide abruptly and out of the blue.

Early musings can look something like this. School leaders find themselves asking: *How is my school positioned for the years to come? Where is it strong and where is it weak? What are its most distinctive commitments and most important offerings? We already stand for much; how can we stand for more?* Such thoughts commonly surface at the natural breakpoints of the educational year. The year is winding down, perhaps with the last faculty meeting. Nothing needs to be decided or even announced, but certainly what the next year will look like, or the year after that, is on people's minds.

Or an academic year is just beginning. The established mechanisms are rolling smoothly into motion. The first faculty meeting comes next week. Again, nothing needs to be decided or even announced. But perhaps this is a good year to begin exploring informally how to take the school forward, toward an on-the-ground initiative the following year.

Or perhaps it's the school holidays. Yes, you're stepping back, but also looking forward. Perhaps this is a moment to consider beginning a process of tinkering with the general direction of things. A modest conversation with a couple of colleagues, with a school board member, with key faculty, might spark some early vision of possibilities.

Or perhaps some group is convening a cross-school conversation for what might be done—this is one of the many roles Independent Schools Victoria has played so effectively. Who knows where the conversation will go, but participating for a bit is easy. Let's see what we can learn about it all.

In summary, it doesn't make much sense simply to decide today, "Okay, let's try this LLtM thing I just heard about." There is a personal and conversational process of exploring the possibilities. If that goes well, it's time to move forward in a more structured way.

What's here

The goal of this book is to share what has been learned so far about LLtM that could contribute toward further innovations in education in any setting, for any sort of school, public or private. Here is a preview of what appears in the following pages.

Part I: Pictures of Practice

This part offers several narrative case studies from schools that have undertaken LLtM, sketching the visions they pursued and how the process unfolded. These pictures of practice illustrate how LLtM can take contrasting forms in various settings. What you construct for your institution might be rather different, but we hope that the case studies will give a sense of the possibilities.

You are welcome to read Part I straight through, but it might make more sense to browse, finding a couple of pictures of practice that inform your own situation best. Part I is organized to make this easy: the pictures of practice are independent of one another and can be read in any order.

Part II: Navigating the Journey

These four sections outline key aspects of organizing and leading the LLtM process.

Visions of the Learning that Matters concerns what LLtM visions are like and how to construct them.

Four Leadership Practices introduces and outlines four key dimensions of the LLtM process: creating shared vision, developing collaborative structures, supporting individual development, and protecting and sustaining progress.

The First Months addresses how to get started, a particularly crucial period for LLtM as for any change process.

On the Journey Together offers several broad principles for sustaining collaboration and maintaining momentum.

Part III: Tools and Tips

Here you will find two sections of tools and tips in the form of diagrams and worksheets for school leaders and faculty participants.

The first section includes tools for building and refining visions for learning that matters in ways suited to the institution.

The second section offers tools for leading learning that matters. Strategies for organizing the overall LLtM initiative and tracking its progress appear here.

The Compass

Finally, on the next page is a compass graphic that includes brief definitions of *learning that matters* and *leading learning that matters*. The cardinal points of the compass mark the four leadership practices mentioned under Part II. On your LLtM journey, consider how the four leadership practices could guide the direction of your thinking and practice in leading the learning that matters in your context.

The Compass

Learning that Matters

"How can learning be expanded beyond traditional academic commitments to matter more in learners' lives?"

Leading Learning that Matters

"How can I shape an institution that stays true to its core commitments, thrives as a contemporary center of learning, and contributes to a complex global society?"

Part I
Pictures of Practice

This picture of practice describes Penbank School's focus on connecting students' learning to their interests, and the school structures that support teachers toward a vision of their students as independent, engaged, and collaborative learners.*

Fostering Personal Significance and Passion in Learning

A laser printer and a toolbox filled with a variety of child-sized tools sit in the tinkering station in a corner of a Year 1 classroom. The printer is on a small table, its back panel open. Student Sean peers into the back of the printer, carefully poking around the configurations of screws, panels, knobs, and other components with a pencil.

"I'm trying to figure out what's keeping the fan in," Sean explains, adding that he had earlier removed the back of the printer case by snapping the latch open. His teacher, Lorraine Ford, nods as she listens to him. After a few minutes, Sean stops, points to two screws to the left of the box fan, and tells her, "I think it's these screws keeping the fan in. I've to take them out." Lorraine looks at where he is pointing and asks, "How will you take them out?" Sean pauses, then tells her that he'll "try to work around it to find out."

Lorraine observes Sean fiddling with the screws for a while before asking, "What do you think you can use to try to get that out?" Sean looks up, thinks for a moment, and then rummages in the toolbox. "I'm using this," he tells Lorraine triumphantly, waving a screwdriver in his hand.

Sean tries to get the slot-head of the screwdriver into the heads of the Phillips screws; they do not budge. After a while, he looks up and tells Lorraine that the screwdriver "doesn't fit here. See?" He points to the tip of the screwdriver and then to the back of the screws. "I've to find another one that fits." He returns to the toolbox and finally finds the correct screwdriver. After working intensely for a few minutes, Sean looks up excitedly and tells Lorraine, "It's out! It's out! I got it out!"

* Since the events depicted in this picture of practice, Penbank School has merged with Woodleigh School to become Woodleigh School's Penbank Campus. Woodleigh School's Penbank Campus provides a warm, caring, and secure yet challenging environment for the development of students in all areas of social responsibility and intellectual learning.

It's about personalizing their learning…so that you involve the children in the curriculum. —*Vivienne Wearne, Deputy Principal*

Students at Penbank learned through investigation and inquiry, in an environment replete with opportunities for them to be the architects of their own learning. Learning centers such as the one that prompted Sean's investigation of the printer reflected the learning that matters at Penbank—learning that engages the students' curiosity and interests.

Deputy Principal Vivienne Wearne explained, "When we look at what it is that's important to them, it's their interests. They have their interests, their passions. So, it's really looking at who these little children are and personalizing their learning, so that you know the children, you involve the children in the curriculum, and you align the curriculum to their interests."

Aligning students' interests with the curriculum began in discussions during the fortnightly teachers' meeting, where teachers planned ways to prep the classrooms and common areas to invite imaginative, independent, and engaged learning. They asked, *What are students currently interested in (e.g., pets, body skeletons, yoga)? What are the school's and community's concerns (e.g., winter explorations of snow and skiing, raising awareness of important issues)? What are the learning targets for the students (e.g., exploring aspects of identity through role-play, understanding and managing emotions, experimentation as problem solving)?*

These decisions, according to teacher Lorraine, resulted in an engaging curriculum for the students and prepared them to be independent, inspired to learn because "they have found their passion coming through the school with all the investigations and Educational Research Projects, something they want to do…and are willing to go out there and have a go at it."

The learning centers at Penbank were designed to nurture dispositional qualities such as independence, curiosity, and self-management of learning. They could be flexibly and differently used by the students, who decided what learning they wanted to embark on, where and how that learning would take place, and whether they were going to learn with others or by themselves.

At the beginning of each investigation session, the teachers discussed the learning intentions for that fortnight with the students, and invited them to consider a few questions: *What do I want to learn? Where do I want to learn? Who do I want to work with? What do I want to do to develop my ideas?*

In the vignette that started this narrative, the learning intention for Sean's class was *How do things work?* Students conducted investigations that explored how camping equipment worked; what cooking implements in an outdoor log kitchen were useful; what a sprawling farm for animals, crops, and recreation looked like; how magnifying glasses could be used to study fossils and bone specimens; and how found materials could be used to create tribal masks.

Such opportunities for independent thinking were especially important, the teachers explained, in an era when computer games and television programs entertained but did not always challenge or provoke thinking.

Lorraine explained the importance of developing students' capacity to think about their learning intentions:

> It's important for them, for their independence, to think for themselves. I think we are heavily into helping our kids as parents, and we don't let them think or do very much for themselves. So when they come to school, it's fantastic that they have the opportunity to start thinking for themselves, and to suffer the consequences, too. Many of us parents try to save them from those experiences. But that doesn't help them.

The teachers at Penbank distinguished explicitly between sparking interest and directing interest. If there was a consistent theme that ran through the learning from Kindergarten to Year 6, it was the laser focus on student interests. While multiple learning centers were created to provoke thinking and learning, students could choose to not use them at all if they decided to follow other interests.

For instance, when a group of students decided that they wanted to pursue different learning

intentions solely through their passion for basketball, the teachers worked with them to frame different lines of inquiry. To learn about materials and their properties, the group explored how the material of the basketball affected the way the game was played, and how the material of basketball jerseys helped or hindered players. They also learned about motion and forces and investigated how these influenced the effectiveness of moves like dribbling, shooting, and passing.

> **It's all from their interests, and that's what's so engaging for them.**
> —Lorraine Ford, teacher

Lorraine explained, "Even though they've been investigating basketball for years, there's always a different aspect that they can look at and learn from; they are still learning the concepts and learning through their interest. It's all from their interests, and that's what's so engaging for them."

Parent volunteer Christina appreciated the teachers' focus on fostering personal significance, commitment, and passion in student learning, and developing students' understanding of academic concepts by building bridges between important content and personal relevance and interests. She explained:

When they [students] move on to secondary school, they'll need to find their passion for learning. As young people, you don't want to just be directed, but in a lot of schools, the direction comes down from the teachers. When those young people have to lead, or use their initiative, it becomes very difficult for them.

The teachers ensured that attending to the students' interests did not compromise the curriculum that had to be taught by paying close attention to what the students were doing and thinking and keeping an eye on students' struggles and misconceptions. They focused each afternoon's subject matter instruction on those struggles and misconceptions to support student learning.

For instance, when Lorraine saw Sean and his peers struggling to explain their ideas in writing, she focused their afternoon lessons on writing informative texts using appropriate text structure, sentence-level grammar, word choice, spelling, punctuation, and supporting illustrations and diagrams. With the older children, teachers designed investigations into the transfer of energy in the morning, and then focused the afternoon's instruction on science concepts related to mass and energy. At all times, the teachers actively searched for opportunities to relate subject matter learning to the students' interests in authentic ways.

How did Penbank create conditions for learning that were driven by student interests? How did the leadership ensure that such conditions were sustained in the face of other competing commitments like examination success?

The vision for the learning that mattered at Penbank was collectively crafted and consistently refined by all the teachers at staff meetings. At one such meeting, Vivienne invited her staff to take stock of that vision: "Let's look back on the dreams that we had previously framed. How do you feel about them now? What do you feel is the learning that really matters to us now?"

After a few minutes of quiet reflection, followed by writing their feelings and thoughts on sticky notes, the faculty shared their notes on the whiteboard and openly discussed the extent to which Penbank as a community had prepared their students for a productive and rewarding life. The school's open, collaborative culture supported such frank conversations, building on a network of strong relationships among staff.

This focus on relationships extended into the classroom: teachers purposefully created opportunities for students to develop positive collaborations and to value teamwork. Vivienne set the tone for that culture by consistently inviting staff to reflect on how they got along with one another as faculty and with their students, as well as reminding students about the importance of teamwork and positive relationships.

Supporting students to be collaborative learners required that the adults in the school modeled what that looked like. For adults and children alike, learning was collaborative, independent, interest-driven, and personally significant. Staff meetings at Penbank were safe and supportive spaces for testing new ideas and discussing challenges. Planning meetings were likewise collaborative, with everyone free to bring up ideas and raise questions.

The staff was also confident that they could go to Vivienne and say, "This is not working. What do you think we can do about it?" They described how Vivienne was always interested in such discussions, responding with "Tell me more about it" and "How do you see that working?" before encouraging them with "That's good, go and do it" or "Let's think about this together."

Integral to that leadership move was Vivienne's commitment to the staff as a learning community; for her, supporting them in their learning was "fundamental because it's the staff that really makes the school tick; they are the ones who need to be excited coming to school every day."

How does one build such a culture? At Penbank, formal structures like staff work days and staff meetings emphasized teamwork, and were planned with that in mind. Informal get-togethers were a running theme in the school, and they promoted conversation and community. The staff had surfed the waves together, regularly enjoyed breakfast together before starting the school day, and got together after work on Fridays just to hang out.

Lorraine explained how those experiences as a community had made Penbank more than just a school:

It's more like family. It's more like you've friends. You have friends here in school. We make time to meet outside of school hours. So it's one team. And Viv encourages that, especially when we have discussions in staff meetings. When we have staff meetings, we sit in a circle, not in rows. It's always a circle.

This picture of practice describes Year 5 students in Overnewton Anglican Community College studying migration as a historical topic and a contemporary issue. Through these lenses, they begin to understand the current refugee crisis and to consider their role in it.†

Learning about Migration, Developing Multiple Perspective-Taking & Empathy

Students Wendy, Irfan, and Mahmud are discussing *The Happiest Refugee*, the autobiographical account of writer Anh Do's experience fleeing Vietnam with his family and arriving in Australia as a refugee.

Irfan: I wonder how Anh Do felt when he first came to Australia. About things like making friends or going out and all. I mean, he doesn't look like everyone else, he didn't feel like everyone else. He wrote about that, that he felt left out of things.

Mahmud: I think I know how Anh Do felt because I came to Australia when I was only three and didn't know any English. I went to kindergarten and the teacher was telling me something, but I didn't understand her. It was very scary!

Irfan: My grandma came as a refugee and she had to stay at a detention centre. But she got sick, so they had to put her in a better detention centre. But it was still a detention centre.

Wendy: My dad came away from Vietnam because life was bad there. But it was also hard here at first. My dad always said it helped that he had his family with him.

Mahmud: But not everyone has that. Many refugees now in Australia don't have their family. And the media says bad things about them and people get so angry that they are here.

Wendy: Especially during the election year. The politicians make it sound much worse just to get votes. My dad said something the other day about how he met people who think Australia should just make all the refugees leave.

Irfan: Oh, really? Can they do that?

Mahmud: That's not fair! How can they just make people leave?

Wendy: Can we change that? How can we change that?

† Overnewton Anglican Community College opened in 1987 in response to a community need for accessible quality education. The college seeks to nurture a community of learners embracing the future, and prepares students to serve as empowered, thoughtful, community-minded citizens.

Anything that the students learn has to be about what's going to help them be a better person. —*Leanne Schulz, teacher*

Overnewton Anglican Community College teacher Leanne Schulz smiled as she recalled the culminating project of the unit, Stories of Migration, during which her Year 5 students not only wrote stories of immigration experiences but also put together suitcases that accompanied the stories. Pointing to one of the suitcases, she explained how she changed the usually straightforward unit on 19th century colonial Australia so that her students could learn about and understand different perspectives on migration and connect their learning to the current global refugee crisis.

While students still did the usual work of researching aspects of 19th century colonial Australia, Leanne's redesigned unit invited them to embark on a series of explorations into the significance of migration in the past as well as in contemporary society. Students considered wider applications of the topic well beyond typical textbook applications. In the unit, students came to understand migration as a multifaceted issue: *How do different people experience migration? What are the multiple push and pull factors for migrating, and how has migration impacted origin countries and receiving communities? Who are the refugees, and why should we care about them?*

Supporting students in grappling with issues like migration and the refugee crisis mattered greatly to Leanne because "these migration stories are real. They are happening in the world, and young people need to be empathetic, to think critically and creatively about things without being narrow-minded." The learning in school must, she argued, develop in students a more expansive view of the world and a more ethical stance vis-à-vis the issues they encounter and study, so that they "become a better person and live their lives with strong morals and a sense of perspective, a sense of deep understanding about what's going on around them."

Maths and science are important, but you need to know what's going on around you and what people are going through. —*Bridgette, student*

The Stories of Migration unit provided rich learning experiences for students to explore key concepts in history (e.g., continuity and change, cause and effect), as well as historical ways of thinking (e.g., using sources, taking perspective, uncovering the significance of events and people in bringing about change). It also extended the business-as-usual way of teaching history by foregrounding the contemporary and the regional, i.e., *What is the refugee crisis in the world today, and how is it impacting Australia and Australians?*

Because she wanted her students to see history not as merely a collection of other people's stories from long ago but as narratives that have powerful resonance with their lives, Leanne brought into the classroom the real-life accounts of past and current refugees in Australia. Her students read the biography of highly popular Australian comedian Anh Do, heard from a young Afghan refugee who visited their class to share her story, and engaged in discussion with a parent who had arrived in Australia after fleeing Vietnam in the 1980s.

Leanne interwove those narratives with key events in Australian history. Her students learned about the utopian notion of "white Australia" and the restrictions that were placed on migrants to Australia in the 1800s, in particular how the government subjected them to the dictation test, which comprised fifty words that were highly unlikely for some groups of migrants to know. The students learned that if the migrants managed to pass the dictation test, they had to take it again in a different European language. One student was bewildered that a government policy could be designed to ensure that the migrants would fail the test and therefore would not be able to stay.

In teaching the unit, Leanne took care not to present a simple, singular picture of the issue. As her students were reporting their astonishment over the narrow-minded views of the people then, she made sure to discuss with them the reasons for why such thinking had been prevalent, particularly what the fears were about migrants at that time:

> *When teaching this unit, it's always about looking at perspectives, not just that this is the way it is. In no way am I saying, "This is what the refugees are all about. Let's get the definition down. This is how it works. This is what happened." We are just exploring together, questioning, wondering, and trying to make a difference. We are not saying that you must learn these as just facts; we are saying you must think about these, because it's important for us and to our world and for the future.*

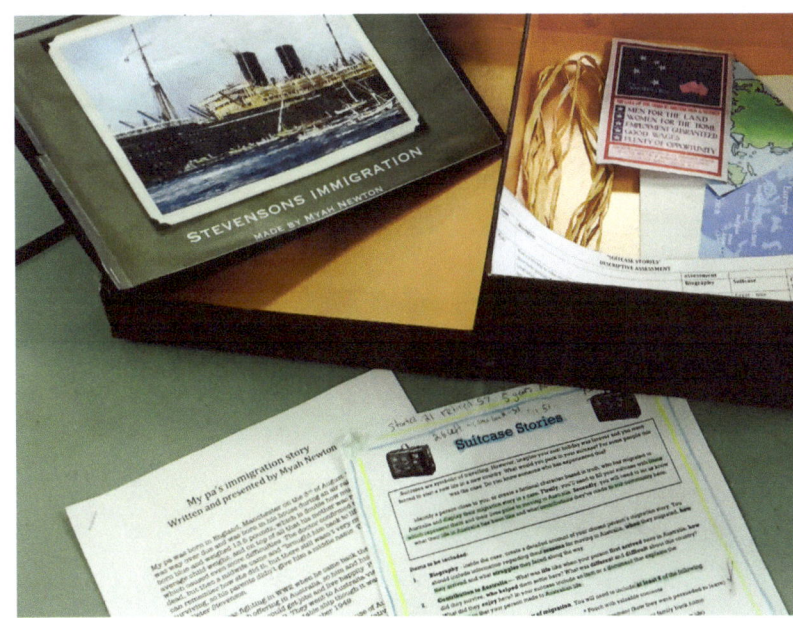

When students like Irfan, Mahmud, and Wendy started to ask questions about migration and the refugee crisis—*Did that really happen? How did it happen? How can people do that? Why do they think that? What can we do? How can we change that?*—they demonstrated the capacity to see history less as a factual account and more as a constructed narrative, to empathize with others, and to see themselves as capable of contributing to how the world might be or should be.

Leanne remembered how during the first few lessons, the students had told her that they didn't know much about migration, nor were they particularly interested in the topic. Now, "all of them have an opinion or idea about it." That opinion about migration and the refugee crisis in Australia came across strongly when student Bridgette shared how, for her, watching TV now felt different:

It makes you think about what you have just learned, about how the media might not always tell the truth. We've learned lots about the policy of migrants and refugees coming to Australia, and how they treat refugees now. It's good to see both sides of the story. When you study about it, you actually realize why they want to come to Australia, and how they feel. And you want to help the people in that situation. Maths and science are important but you need to know what's going on around you and what people are going through.

The culminating project of the Stories of Migration unit required students to create a suitcase story, modeled after the immigration suitcases at the Immigration Museum in Melbourne. Each immigration suitcase contained objects, artifacts, and documents that told a specific story of how a non-Indigenous person arrived on the shores of Australia. As a collection, the immigration suitcases revealed the rich history and cultural diversity of those who make up Australia today.

Leanne borrowed one of the suitcases from the museum and used it to explore the following questions with the students: *Who were the people who left their country? Why did they leave? What was their migration journey like? How have they contributed to our country? How has our country changed over time?* From there, Leanne created opportunities for the students to develop their knowledge of mapping conventions and apply that understanding to the creation and analysis of maps.

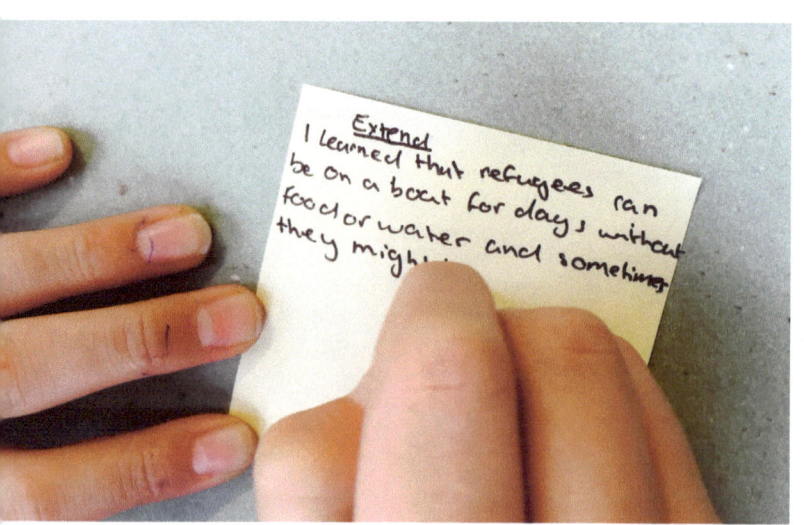

Finally, the students were tasked with interviewing someone they knew who had migrated to Australia. They had to craft their own interview questions to gather enough information for a compelling narrative and then present that narrative using text and artifacts. In a reflection task, students had to consider how the personal artifacts belonging to their interviewee contributed to a rich story of migration. The unit wrapped up with a public exhibition of the students' suitcase stories.

Teaching the Stories of Migration unit required adequate time for the learning arc to play out, yet time is usually in short supply in schools. How did Leanne carve out the chunk of time needed to teach the unit as envisioned? While Leanne acknowledged that there was a considerable range of things every teacher had to get through in a semester, she nonetheless believed that curricular choices had to be anchored in what mattered most for students to learn:

> *You don't stop just because, oops, time's up. I think everything in this unit is valuable, so I plan and make sure I do it well. You have a whole term. In between, of course, you must do your science and your maths and your reading, but you have to allow time for thinking. That's how students will value their learning. They don't think, you've ticked that, and I've done that. Or asking whether they have a test on that. It's about each step, growing, building, consolidating, and then doing something with their learning. This sort of learning will stay with them*

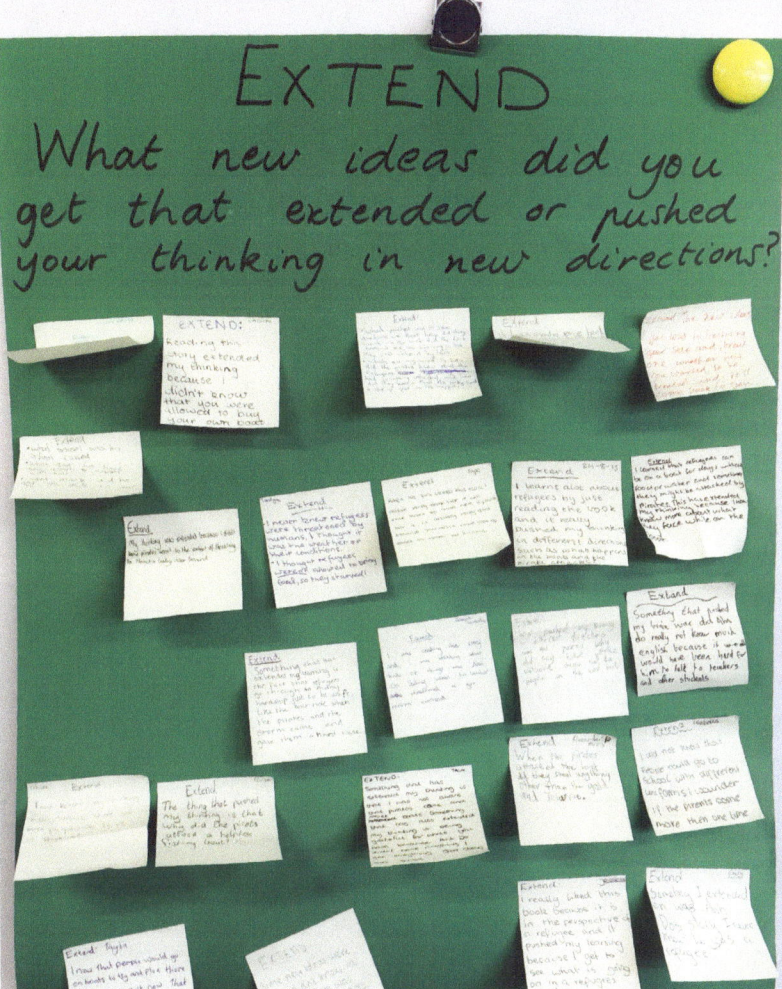

forever. The date of the immigration scheme doesn't matter. It's the big ideas, the big concepts, the life lessons, their empathy, the connections, seeing different perspectives. That's the learning that matters.

Leanne was not alone in her conviction that topics that were worth learning demanded time for students to explore and think. Janet Jolley, Head of the Middle School, similarly emphasized the importance of creating a thinking culture in the classroom and encouraged teachers to take calculated risks in their teaching towards that end, even if it meant making decisions to focus less time on some traditional curricular topics:

> At no stage do we dictate that a unit has to be like this, or that you must do this now and you must do that then. Instead we have a framework and a set of guidelines for people to work with. While the curriculum is clearly documented, it's not Day 1, Day 2, Day 3…. Instead, it offers flexibility, and that flexibility within a set framework enables teachers to create, to innovate, to spend time on what's important.

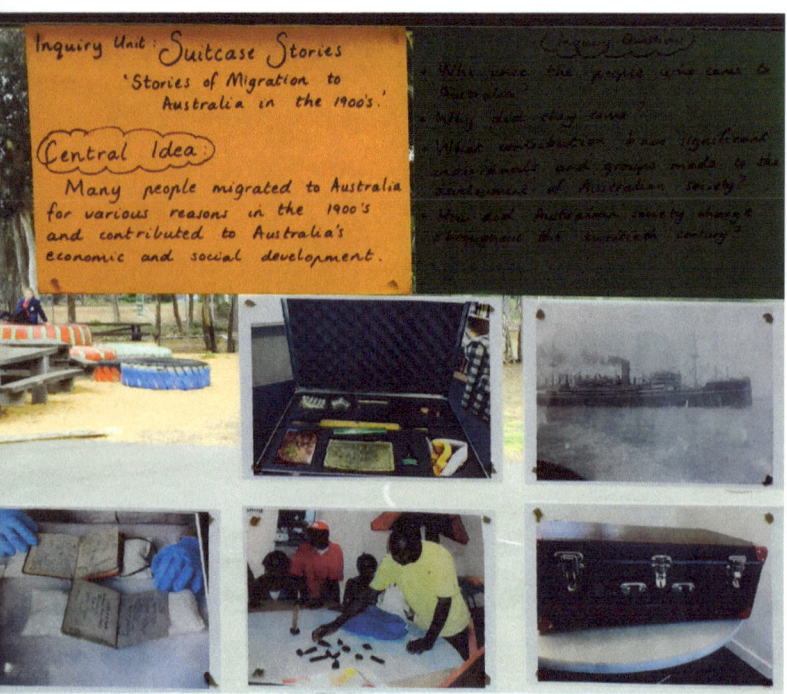

Leanne also valued the opportunity for the entire Middle School staff to sign up for online professional development courses offered by Harvard-Project Zero because it was instrumental in getting all teachers on the same page about pedagogical philosophy and ideas: "Now it's more effective and efficient to have open discussions about what and how we teach because we share similar understandings and philosophies."

Principal Jim Laussen saw the Middle School teachers' participation in the Harvard-Project Zero online programs as a logical evolution of the Middle School's focus on the learning that matters, because the staff had already been doing work with thinking routines and other strategies to support student learning. It built on what was already happening, and he believed if you wanted an initiative to be powerful in your school, you built on something that was already there.

How did the school leader support the staff toward the learning that mattered, especially when it meant restructuring established practices? For Jim, the touchstone was ensuring coherence and alignment across the school, beginning with "long conversations with your leadership team and saying, ok, what are the key objectives? What are the things we've been working on in each of our areas at the moment? And making sure that whatever you do, you tie those pieces together; otherwise they're not going to take root. People will just say, here's one more thing we've got to do."

To ensure that the focus on the learning that mattered took root across the school, Jim revamped the leadership team and its practices. First, he recognized the inefficiency of a large leadership team of eighteen people and divided it into two teams, each with a clearly delineated role—one team was responsible for operational matters in the college (e.g., policy, finances, management, etc.), while the other focused purely on academic matters.

Next, he created a cascading system of instructional leadership: since the heads of school were the ones driving what was going on in their school, he initiated a regular monthly check-in with them on the learning going on in each school, and the direction that it was taking. Following the meeting, the heads of school brought the ideas back to their teaching and learning committees, and worked with them to support the learning envisioned collectively.

Thirdly, Jim intentionally changed the nomenclature of the instructional leadership in the school, from "Head of *Curriculum*" to "Head of *Learning*," to shift the focus of the leadership from the traditional curricular administration to the learning and teaching happening in the classroom. The College Curriculum Committee also became the College Learning Committee, and Jim regularly attended the committee meetings to more effectively drive change.

For Jim, those changes underscored an important shift in the way he viewed his role in the school. He remembered how in his first twelve years as a principal, he had to learn things about school buildings that he had never thought he would need to know:

[We had] constant building programs going on, and while it was exciting for the community to have new classrooms and learning spaces and so on, it's a distraction from my core business. It's ridiculous. My core business is what's going on in the classroom. It's leading a school, an institution dedicated to the learning of our young people. So, I've forced myself back into the instructional space because if you're going to be the instructional leader, that's what you have to do. You get involved in the learning.

This picture of practice describes a Year 12 literature class at Ivanhoe Girls' Grammar School where students learn to critically appreciate the work of Irish poet Seamus Heaney, in the process developing a thoughtful stance toward messages we frequently encounter in our contemporary society.‡

Exploring Literature as a Lens on the World and the Self

In their Year 12 literature class, students Arlie, Suhadi, and Erin discuss the ideas and emotions evoked by the language that Irish poet Seamus Heaney used in his poem "Limbo."

Suhadi: The word "spawning" in the line "An illegitimate spawning" really catches my attention… because when you read "spawning," you think of fish or frogs or animals. Not human babies.

Erin: Yes, it's also in "Death of a Naturalist." [She shuffles through several pages, finds the poem, and reads.] "The daddy frog was called a bullfrog / And how he croaked and how the mammy frog / Laid hundreds of little eggs and this was / Frogspawn." Makes me think of devil spawn!

Suhadi: Yes, there's kind of disgust in "spawning," like the dead baby is something dirty or gross.

Arlie: But there's also something sad about the dead baby in the lines "Netted… / Along with the salmon." I think juxtaposing the baby with the salmon is important. Is the illegitimate baby of an unwed woman unwanted and disgusting, or just sad and pitiful? Also, whose voice or perspective is that—Heaney's or Catholic Ireland's?

Erin: Yes! Reading the words literally, it's comparing the dead baby to fish eggs. But connecting it to the later lines about the mother "ducking him tenderly" into the water… she was dipping him, like baptizing him in the water, and it changes the feeling totally, doesn't it?

Arlie: Yet the dead baby is described as in limbo, like stuck in Purgatory or something. Do the loving actions of the mother redeem it? At the end of the poem, the baby is "hauled in with the fish." That's really heartbreaking!

Suhadi: There are more and more layers to this poem as we dig deeper!

‡ Ivanhoe Girls' Grammar School is an independent Anglican day school for girls established in 1903 with the aim of providing the best learning and teaching that, underpinned by the Christian philosophy, enables every girl to achieve her potential and to be a confident, optimistic, and responsible citizen.

> **We always talk about what is the best learning for our girls, and what they need for their future lives…[to be] articulate, courageous, critical thinkers who are generous of spirit, have a life-long love of learning, and who have a voice and use it to create change.** —*Heather Schnagl, Principal*

Prominently displayed on a banner over the Principal's Message on the school's website was the statement, "Our girls speak for themselves." At Ivanhoe Girls' Grammar School, nurturing students to become young women who were confident, critical, and independent thinkers was at the heart of its educational mission. Aligned with that mission, three questions guided the school's curricular discussions and decisions: *To what extent will this contribute to the holistic development of our girls? Does it support our students to understand themselves as learners? How do we ensure that they feel safe and confident in their ability to pursue deep learning?* For Principal Heather Schnagl, these questions were critical:

The best learning for our girls, what they need for their future lives, is all the things that make them a whole person—academic, emotional, spiritual, values, character. When they have all that, they can chart their life forward, they have the skills and confidence to achieve their individual goals. And they are articulate, courageous, critical thinkers who are generous of spirit, have a life-long love of learning, and who have a voice and use it to create change.

Intentional efforts to nurture that "voice" were unmistakable in the literature curriculum designed by Head of English Madeleine Coulombe for the Year 11-12 classes. Madeleine saw the Year 11-12 literature curriculum as a rich opportunity to support the intellectual and personal growth of students by building bridges between important disciplinary content and the students' interests and commitments. Recognizing that her students entered their final two years in the school with a deep curiosity about and appreciation for the complexities and issues that they frequently encountered in the media, Madeleine planned her literature lessons to be supportive spaces for grappling with emerging ideas and questions.

The texts that Madeleine selected for her classes not only challenged the students to interrogate writers' theories about important themes, ideas, and contexts, but also invited them to rigorously examine their own lived experiences, their communities, and the world. For instance, Henrik Ibsen's *A Doll's House* raised questions for students about what it meant to be a woman in a traditional and male-dominated society; Jane Austen's *Pride and Prejudice* presented them with complex and often challenging social mores—ambition, expectations, marriage, class, taboos—that young women, whether in late 18th century England or 21st century Australia, had to navigate; and Seamus Heaney's poetry highlighted tensions that brewed between the individual and the citizen, as well as one's personal identity and other affiliations.

In Madeleine's class, students were given ample time to sit with the texts to understand the perspectives presented and to develop an informed personal stance vis-à-vis the themes presented in the texts. They were also encouraged to critically evaluate and thoughtfully express their ideas, however divergent they might be from their peers'. In the process, they built confidence and courage in their capacity to grapple with complex and often fraught issues.

A common sight in Madeleine's literature classroom was students bent over a set of texts scribbling their thoughts on paper. At other times, the students worked in small groups discussing their ideas about the texts with their peers. Madeleine assigned her students to work through each text systematically: they first identified the linguistic devices employed by the writers, and then probed carefully and deeply into how those devices conveyed rich and often nuanced meanings. At all times, the students were invited to grapple with how the language simultaneously evoked and repressed, suggested and dissuaded, revealed and evaded.

To develop the level of thoughtful response she hoped to see from her students, Madeleine selected texts that were developmentally appropriate and optimally challenging for her students. She believed that they should be inducted into texts that they would not normally choose to read, as well as texts that presented challenges within their zone of proximal development. That way, she hoped that they would develop the confidence to

go out and feel they can read anything. When I'm selecting texts in Year 11 and 12, I do want to choose texts that will push boundaries a little bit and that are a little bit more difficult. They should be difficult; that's why we are studying them. And the class will provide the mentoring for them to understand how to read, so that they can encounter other texts without fear.

In her experience, a fruitful way to help students manage the complexity and richness of the texts they read was through the close reading and annotation they did in class. Students were asked to analyze each text through several lenses—narrative or literal, literary qualities, mechanics, connections—and discuss how the different lenses created a textured and layered narrative that evoked nuanced interpretations. Madeleine saw the literary methods of close reading and annotation as

developing a relationship with or being in conversation with different texts. It's not a one-off thing; you read the text, go out and

Literature is deeply revealing of not only the writer or poet's world and view, but also of how we see who we are, and what our world is like today. It helps me really look hard and deeply into myself and my world, and I find myself confronting questions like: *Who am I, and who do I want to be? How do I get there, and does my community and the world allow me to get there?* —Erin, student

live your life, and then you come back, and you are in relationship or conversation with it again. And you do it again and again, so it becomes intricately woven into the fabric of your life. I don't think that runs counter to our lives now. I think that more than ever we are asked to be in relationship with or respond to a whole variety of texts throughout our lives every day, coming in through all different kinds of sources.

For the students in Madeleine's Year 12 literature class, studying the poetry of Seamus Heaney went beyond acquiring a working knowledge of the literary canon; it prepared them to skillfully uncover the multiple messages conveyed in texts and to develop an informed view of how the world is presented, in the past and today. As they read Heaney's poems, the students asked themselves: *What is happening in the poems narratively? What do the words and phrases call to mind, and how many levels of meaning can we see? What connections to other ideas, events, contexts, etc., are possible, and can we make a case for those connections? How is each poem significant for the poet and his audience, and how are they significant and relevant to us today?* By inviting her students to engage with the poems analytically, critically, and personally, Madeleine's lessons empowered them to go well beyond textbook applications of the learning. Student Arlie explained:

> We're looking at the poetry not just in terms of Heaney's context like his beliefs, political affiliations, and the political situation at that time; we are really digging deeply into the way he uses language, the motifs and connections across his poems throughout his career.... The act of analyzing language really carries you in life; it's one of the most important skills you'll have. I realize now that I don't want to just consume media passively. I want to be really active and analytical, to understand how I am being manipulated as a reader and what a writer is trying to make me think. I think that's key, in political as well as just general recreational reading.

When Madeleine's students were invited to reflect on how each text they studied in the classroom was relevant to their personal lives, the learning came alive for them in vivid and important ways. They reported that the texts helped them not only to see connections across the collection of literary works they had been reading, but, more significantly, resonated with the emerging questions that they found themselves asking about who they were and where they were going. Student Erin described how literature had become a window into the world and into herself:

> Literature is deeply revealing of not only the writer or poet's world and view, but also of how we see who we are, and what our world is like today. It helps me really look hard and deeply into myself and my world, and I find myself confronting questions like: Who am I, and who do I want to be? How do I get there, and does my community and the world allow me to get there? If the answer is no, what do I do? In two years, I'll be in the university, and these are such important questions to start asking myself.

Madeleine recognized how well-selected literature texts could be great "teachers" for her students because her own experience had taught her the value of language in shaping ourselves, our world, and our future. She fondly recalled how the novel *A Man for All Seasons*, which she had read in high school, stayed with her very deeply and changed her ethically and morally as a person:

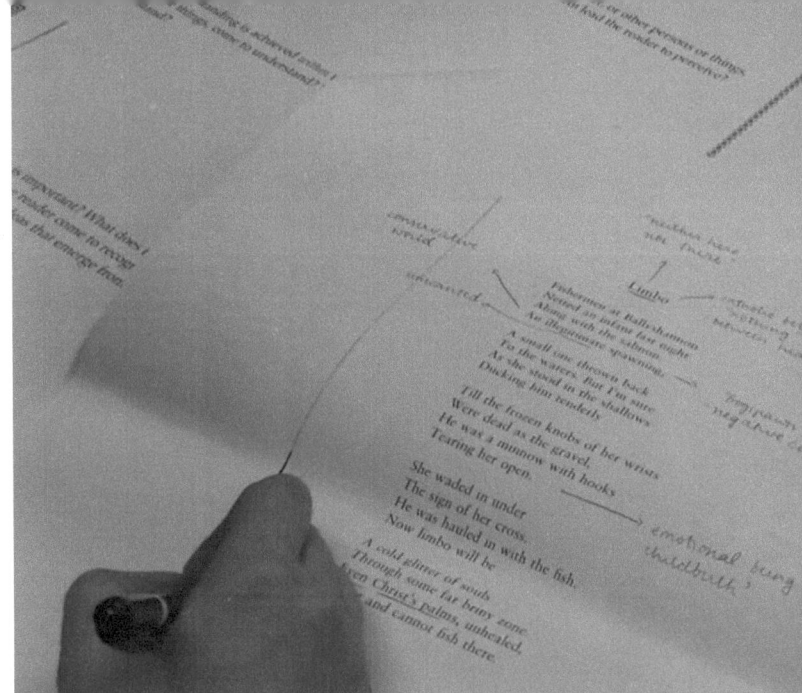

> Thirty years from now, they may not remember exactly what they studied, but they'll remember those larger ideas and things and concepts and be affected by them. Sometimes it's rejecting what is in the text as well. I mean you don't want them to go out and think like Richard III! The questions that guide what we do in the literature classroom should be: What do we endorse? What do we reject? What do we challenge?

Ivanhoe Girls' Grammar School's commitment to helping the students find their own voices extended to the staff. Principal Heather Schnagl made it a point to encourage and empower her staff to take calculated risks in their teaching to achieve the school's mission. When Madeleine decided to have her students "step outside of the curriculum for a time" to work on autobiographical projects so that they had the time and space to reflect on their journeys as

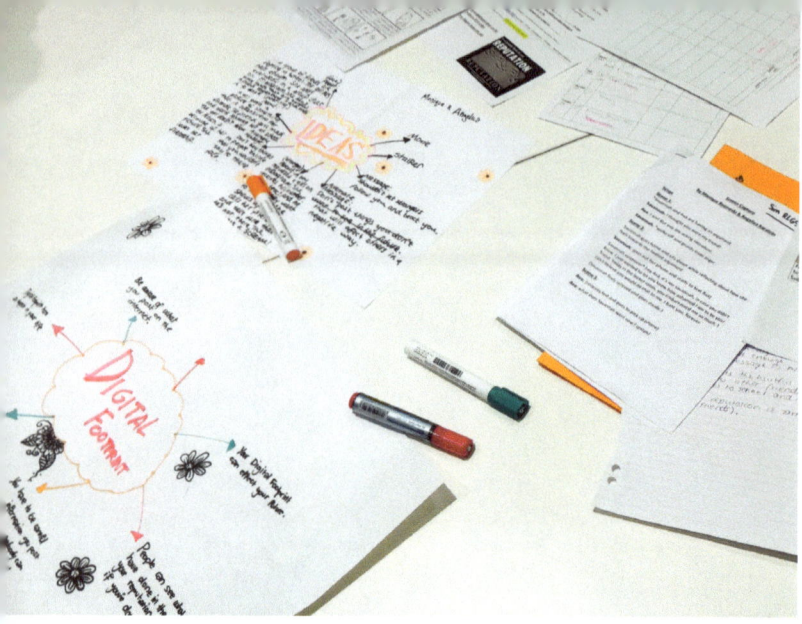

readers and writers, Heather supported her decision because she trusted Madeleine's belief that taking time out of the official curriculum was crucial for students in the arc of their learning.

Having that space for introspection resulted in the students finding resonances with their peers' reflections and deepening their understanding of literature as a discipline, including the dispositions necessary for success as a reader and writer. In order to still meet the demands of the state examination, Madeleine reworked the syllabus to spend less time on another unit that she could abbreviate without compromising the students' learning.

Heather recognized such calculated risks as evidence of teachers' agency and considered professional judgment: as leaders of the learning in their disciplinary areas, the teachers should be able to gauge the learning needs of their students and plan accordingly. She emphasized that

backing them to the hilt is important, because there will be parents saying that their children did not get the usual holiday homework or did not study this book or that film that last year's class did. I tell those parents that I absolutely trust what the team has asked the girls to do. I trust that it is absolutely better for their daughter. Knowing that I will back them encourages my staff to take those necessary risks for the learning that matters.

At the same time, Heather cautioned that one had to be prepared to talk through such decisions with the teachers, especially if there were warning signs that the students' learning could be compromised. This delicate balancing act of empowering yet maintaining oversight was a challenge that Heather saw as an important leadership move that also functioned as a way of developing her staff:

In Australia, there's still the selection into tertiary institutions, and if it doesn't work for that, it's not going to help the girls. That's the dialogue I have with the teachers. The Head of Learning and Teaching meets with them regularly, and I meet with the teachers two or three times a year to hear what they see as the challenges for their department and where they see it's going. So it's an agreed-upon direction but it's also empowering them to make on-the-ground decisions. You've to hire the very best, but you also have to keep helping them grow. The culture we encourage is an important part of it, the empowering culture. I always tell the staff, "I'll back you to the hilt publicly, but there may be a time that we'll need to have a conversation when I think you've made a mistake, but that'll be privately."

Focusing the school on the learning that matters has taken Heather much longer than she had initially expected. The process of making the necessary changes and building the curriculum team hit unexpected road bumps when the staff focused myopically on issues such as timetabling, room assignments, individual teacher duties, and teaching load. Over time, Heather and her leadership team helped the curriculum leaders realize that as curriculum leaders of the school, they were responsible for making really important structural decisions:

Giving them a sense of how all the different parts of the school work together towards the whole picture has done the massive job of broadening their view of the whole entity, and so they move away from the solo view. That's a real problem in secondary schools, the solo disciplinary view. We've broken it down; we haven't got there yet, but we've made progress.

For Heather, sustaining such hard-won progress required that she and her staff consistently fall back on the questions, *What is the thing that's most important now? What are we going to do, and what are we not going to do?* Asking those questions meant that she did not always get to move ahead on initiatives that had initially seemed sensible. For instance, the school intentionally decided not to have a separate Year 9 campus and not to offer the International Baccalaureate program because having the cohort of girls in their final years of school together in one space was a far better way for them to learn to support their peers.

Another conscious decision centered on introducing new languages into the curriculum. Instead of allowing a plethora of language options, Heather and her team decided to offer a more streamlined program. Two languages were offered, French and Chinese, beginning in the primary school through Year 12. That meant that students learned in large communities with more opportunities to practice and interact with their peers. Heather saw such deliberate, carefully thought-out decisions as critical paving stones for enduring change:

If a school tries to do five or more different languages, it gets expensive. You end up with five or six students doing each one, and you miss out on a critical mass. So it's a deliberate decision to just have an Asian and a European language. I never want to be in a situation where there's a whole series of fads and nothing gets embedded. I have had to be really conscious about my decisions. Some of the things I really want to do, I've had to wait for the right time, the right place, to do.

This picture of practice describes how lower secondary students at Westbourne Grammar School developed a growth mindset through regular opportunities to reflect on their learning and interrogate what resilience looked like and how it played a role in their learning and the future lives they envisioned.§

Developing Reflective Capacity and Resilience through Self-Managed Learning

Below is an excerpt from Year 9 student Sam's Presentation of Learning (POL), where he shared with his peers what he had learned from working on a group project to improve the recovery of elderly patients in the local hospital's aged-care facilities.

> Well, I have found my group to be an absolute godsend. We've been able to work really well together even though we didn't really know each other at the start of the year. We've been able to complete a project that went on throughout the year, and to do it well.
>
> Through working on the project, I've learned how emotionally depressed people in aged-care facilities can get. Through our research, we found that across the country as a whole, men and women aged 85-plus were more likely than any other demographic to commit suicide. It shows how quickly the quality of our life can deteriorate not only physically but also emotionally as we age, and if we can do something about that, we should.
>
> Also, I hadn't realized the lengthy process it takes to rehabilitate an elderly person with that level of physical and emotional fragility back to good health and help them integrate back into their community.
>
> Personally, I've become more collaborative and better at communicating with others. At the beginning of the year, I wasn't the best collaborative worker, nor were my communication skills with people outside of my peer group particularly good or useful because I wasn't able to get my ideas across to them clearly or properly. Working with people in the Williamstown aged-care unit on this project, and having to communicate with them and get my ideas across more effectively, has helped me become better not only in working in a group but also in communicating with others.
>
> I have also become more creative because I've had to think about how to use the science of colour to achieve our desired outcomes in the aged-care room. Going forward, I think being more creative, collaborative, and communicative will make me successful in the future, not just in the short term, but definitely in the next twenty, thirty years.

§ Westbourne Grammar School is an independent and non-denominational Christian co-educational day school spread over two campuses. The school's philosophy rests on the foundation of a strong moral purpose and affirms that every child can succeed and achieve significant growth.

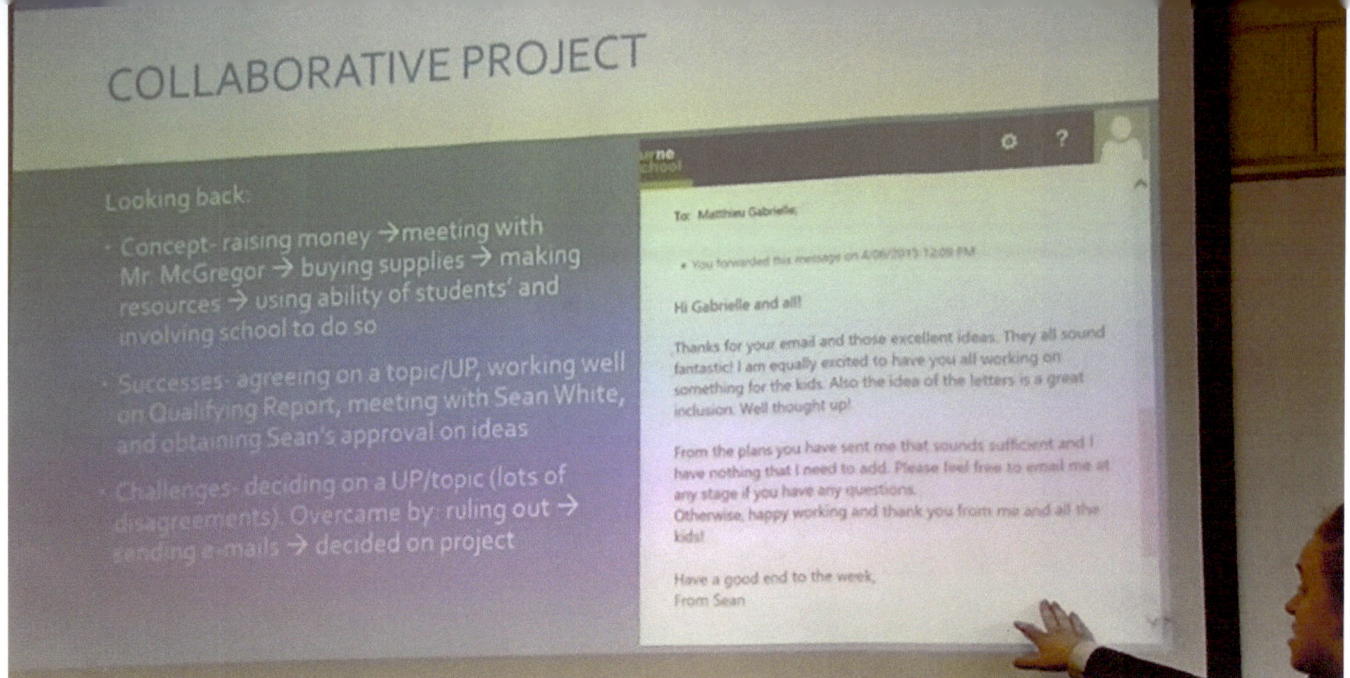

Extended group projects like the one that student Sam described in his Presentation of Learning were a defining feature of the Year 9 Imagine Program at Westbourne Grammar School. The Imagine Program built upon the premise that "teenagers have the capacity to rigorously and passionately explore learning themes and relationships with others." The program organized students into small groups and challenged them to identify opportunities for taking positive action in their community. The projects that the groups undertook not only supported their learning of core disciplinary concepts relevant to a particular problem or issue, but also nurtured important capacities that prepared them well for work and life in today's dynamic and demanding world.

Sam's group chose to investigate why the rehabilitation of elderly patients in a local hospital was not achieving the level of success hoped for and proposed ways to change that. They conducted interviews with the patients and hospital staff, studied successful programs in other healthcare facilities that reported high recovery rates with similar populations, and brainstormed ideas for tackling the problem. Finally, they landed on using the psychology of color to inexpensively but effectively transform the recovery room where elderly patients go each day for meals and to interact with one another.

The students learned important competencies such as collaborating with others, even if that meant stepping out of their comfort zone. Sam ruefully remembered how he was initially skeptical about working with others in a group:

I was always better off working on my own because I could control the workflow and manage the quality of the work. I guess I didn't really trust that other people would do as good a job as I could. But that meant that I was really killing myself trying to do everything! When I slowly learned that the other people in my group had skills I didn't have and were really better than me in so many other ways, I had to let go of the control and figure out how to work with them. That's when I realized that working with others made our overall work much, much better than I could have ever done on my own, and that there is so much I could learn from others!

Throughout the project, students managed their own learning through the process of self-reflection in three POLs. The Imagine Project was an important initiative toward realizing Westbourne's vision of developing reflective and thoughtful learners who recognized the value of respectful and sustainable relationships with others and sought to build a better world through innovation, originality, and generative problem-solving.

The POL process required that students complete three public presentations that reflected on their learning during the school year. The first 15-minute POL—explaining what they understood learning to be, how they learned best, and what they needed to get better at in order to learn best—took place after the students had completed a Visual Oral Reading Kinesthetic questionnaire to diagnose their strengths and weaknesses in learning. The next POL lasted half an hour, and the presenting student's task was to teach the class something. The final POL was 45 minutes long, and provided a clear window into how the student had benefitted from the group project and what additional steps were necessary to move the project forward.

Each POL offered the presenting students opportunities to gather feedback from their teacher and peers. Sam's classmate Brigitte worked on a project collecting resources for the RSPCA (Royal Society for the Prevention of Cruelty to Animals) to improve the lives of abandoned animals, and she remembered how nerve-racking her first POL was:

> *I was just really shaking because I didn't think I could just stand in front of my classmates and describe my weaknesses for fifteen minutes! I mean, aren't we always trying to hide our flaws? But the feedback I got from everyone was really*

[A growth mindset allows learners to] question without fear, and understand that success is not a destination, but a process of continuing in the knowledge that failure is not fatal, but rather an opportunity to move forward more purposefully and with insight. —Meg Hansen, *Principal*

helpful; there were many interesting ways to overcome my weaknesses that I hadn't thought about. Also it turned out that I wasn't the only one with those flaws! Now I really value feedback, and I'm more confident about admitting that I don't always know the best way to do something, or to admit that I'm not that good at something. I feel I've become more resilient from doing the POLs, that when things don't go my way, I don't fall apart, that I can find ways to improve. I can look at myself and figure out why I didn't succeed at something, and how I can do it better the next time.

For Principal Meg Hansen, resilience and capacity for self-reflection were the learning that mattered for the students at Westbourne, especially in an era of ever-increasing social, technological, and cultural change and complexity. While recognizing the exciting promise and possibilities that awaited young people in contemporary society, Meg was also keenly aware of the importance of nurturing in students the capacities that would stand them in good stead in a future that was largely unknown:

For our students, their world will be one that is full of promise. Choice and possibility will exist on a scale unprecedented in human history. Globalisation will continue apace and, increasingly, more will be expected of our young people. Because many of them will be working in jobs that do not yet exist, it will be deep-level thinking, creativity, and imagination that become fundamental skills. Their ability to use knowledge in new situations will position them for a workplace increasingly focused on making the most of information rather than just knowing facts.

Meg recognized that a growth mindset underpinned those capabilities and allowed learners to "question without fear, and understand that success is not a destination, but a process of continuing in the knowledge that failure is not fatal, but rather an opportunity to move forward more purposefully and with insight."

Teacher and Year 9 Director Dennis Nowak similarly described the Imagine Program as a targeted initiative to develop a range of critical 21st century skills that would not only positively impact student learning, but also develop in students the disposition for lifelong learning. For him, Year 9 was the optimal moment in the students' learning journey to begin to develop the kind of high-level metacognition; deeper, sustained, and creative thinking; problem-finding; and problem-solving necessary for success today because developmentally the students were beginning to realize how the world was a much bigger and more complex place than they had imagined:

What we really want to see is that at the end of Year 12, our students are resilient, passionate, enthusiastic, and curious. So we start in Year 9 with these POLs so that the students learn how

> **If we expect that our students will learn and grow, then they need to be able to see that their teachers are willing to learn and grow. If we believe that our abilities are locked in, then we will also think that the students' abilities are locked in.... We should have high expectations of our students. If we don't, we are simply setting them up for failure.**
> —Dennis Nowak, *Year 9 Director*

to collaborate with others, to reflect on their own learning and start to develop resilience in their learning, and to see that they have the capability to tackle problems and emerge with a clearer sense of how to succeed.

Despite the success of the Imagine Program, implementing it was not always smooth sailing. The mandate that all Year 9 students work in groups on projects that addressed authentic problems was initially met with resistance from both students and parents. Dennis recalled that it actually generated a great deal of angst in the parent community because many parents did not want their children to be assessed based on the performance of their peers. The students were similarly agitated when the program first started because they were fixated on who their group members were going to be and whether those would be people they liked to work with.

The teachers responded to the students' anxieties by using the first term to build positive group dynamics among the cohort, instead of setting up the groups right away. They also focused on creating a positive atmosphere in the classroom using informal student circles that built trust and camaraderie. By the end of the first term, the students were convinced that the teachers had their best interests at heart and really knew what they were doing.

To allay parents' worries, the teachers made it a point to explain the program in full detail to the parent community: the philosophy of the enterprise, the structure of the program, and the model of assessment. They also made themselves readily available to meet with parents who were still anxious.

Perhaps what was most challenging for Dennis in his first year as the director of the program was the "wait it out" attitude of a few teachers on his team. Those teachers saw the program as simply the same old idea repackaged under a new name and thought that all they needed to do was to ride it out, go offline and stay under the radar, keep doing the same old thing, and hopefully no one would notice:

People have really struggled with those changes. You know, changes can be really challenging, especially when you see that the school results

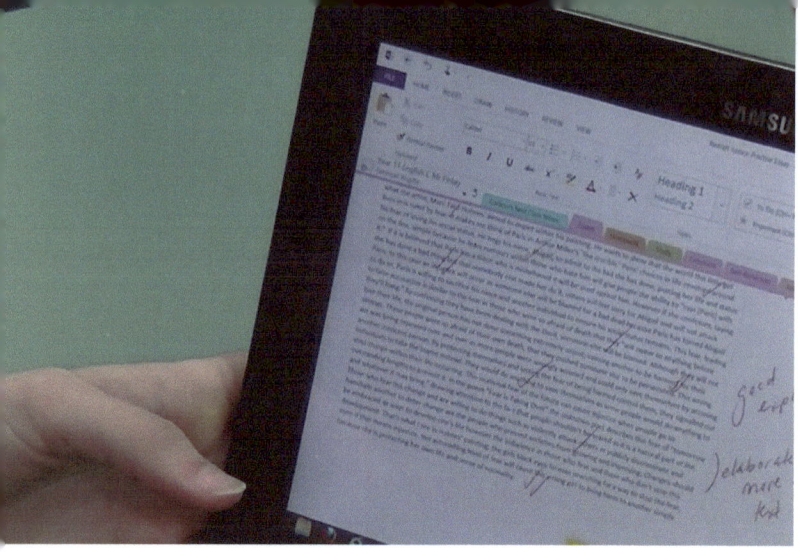

haven't suffered when you were doing the same old thing. Sharing the experience of the change with one another was key; it was important not to let people think that they are struggling alone. So when the team met every Wednesday morning, we kept it honest and shared the steps that we were each taking to get comfortable with it. We just plugged away at it, sharing what we did, spending at least fifteen minutes out of the hour each time sharing best practices and anecdotal stories to try to get people on board.

A year into the Imagine Program, Dennis spoke of his Year 9 teaching team with evident pride, attributing the success of the Imagine Program to their willingness to practice the values and behavior they expected to see in their students:

It's so important that young adults believe that they can get better, and they need to get that from us. If we expect that our students will learn and grow, then they need to be able to see that their teachers are willing to learn and grow. If we believe that our abilities are locked in, then we will also think that the students' abilities are locked in. If we think that, we will not set high expectations or challenge them. Then the students are not going to believe in their own capacity to grow. We should have high expectations of our students. If we don't, we are simply setting them up for failure.

Implementing the Imagine Program as a core initiative in the curriculum meant that a certain level of flexibility with the traditional curriculum had to be possible. Dennis empowered his team to make curricular decisions that put the students at the center of what they did, even if it meant giving less time to one or two topics in the syllabus. For instance, when a cohort of students struggled with understanding slavery as a historical fact and a philosophical concept, he encouraged the teachers to spend more time on the topic rather than rush through it in order to "cover" the curriculum:

We really didn't have to teach the Gold Rush in week 3 just because it's in the curriculum planner. The important consideration is that the students are not understanding this important element of slavery, so what's the point of pushing to get to the Gold Rush if they haven't consolidated what we are talking about at the moment?

When Principal Meg Hansen looked back on the journey of change that she had brought the school on, she identified three key moves that helped her begin to embed the innovation.

First, she made *learning* the core of every endeavor in the school. The agenda of every meeting, whether involving the curriculum leaders, disciplinary teams, or grade-level teachers, focused the conversation on the learning that mattered. When teachers met with the leadership team to discuss their teaching plans, the dialogue centered on learning. Even during whole-school staff meetings, Meg made sure to allocate only ten minutes to policy and administrative matters, insisting that the bulk of the meeting time was spent discussing student learning.

Second, Meg brought the intellectual, emotional, and social well-being of the students into everything that her staff and leadership team discussed and did. For her, everything that they talked about must necessarily involve considering how students were being served well. In fact, she planned to start bringing student voices into staff discussions on student learning because it was important that they had a voice in their own learning:

> *It's important to me that we challenge how we treat one another as humans, whether we are talking about older or younger humans. I remember how as a young learner in school, I was in the top class, but I always felt too frightened to say I didn't understand something. Looking back on that now, I feel strongly that that fear somehow shaved and pruned my capacity and intelligence.*

Third, Meg made communication of the school's initiatives to the staff and parents a priority because keeping them informed recruited them as partners in the endeavor to nurture thoughtful, reflective, and resilient learners. Believing that parents really wanted to know how their children were experiencing school, Meg started holding regular parent information evenings to connect the parents to how the school was supporting the growth of their children. She also launched a parents' portal where parents could log on to browse the academic and professional resources that the teachers and leadership were reading to inform their curricular plans and decisions. Parents could also watch recordings of parent information meetings, submit questions they had, and familiarize themselves with the entire curricular scope and forms of assessment used in the classes. Keeping the channels of information open and inviting, and school decisions transparent, ensured that parents were well-informed, respected, and involved in their children's learning. For Meg, her decisions were guided by the firm belief that every child at school deserved to feel comfortable, secure, and happy:

> *Our students deserve to be engaged in learning in the classroom, to be a vital part of the learning process and not to feel like an outsider, and to be confident that their learning is getting careful attention, and that they are not treated like aliens who have to wait to be part of the real world. They matter now and not just in the future.*

This picture of practice describes how teachers at Xavier College found a way to support their students' interest in computer programming by creating an interest club that offered students opportunities to develop their programming skills while at the same time serving their community.

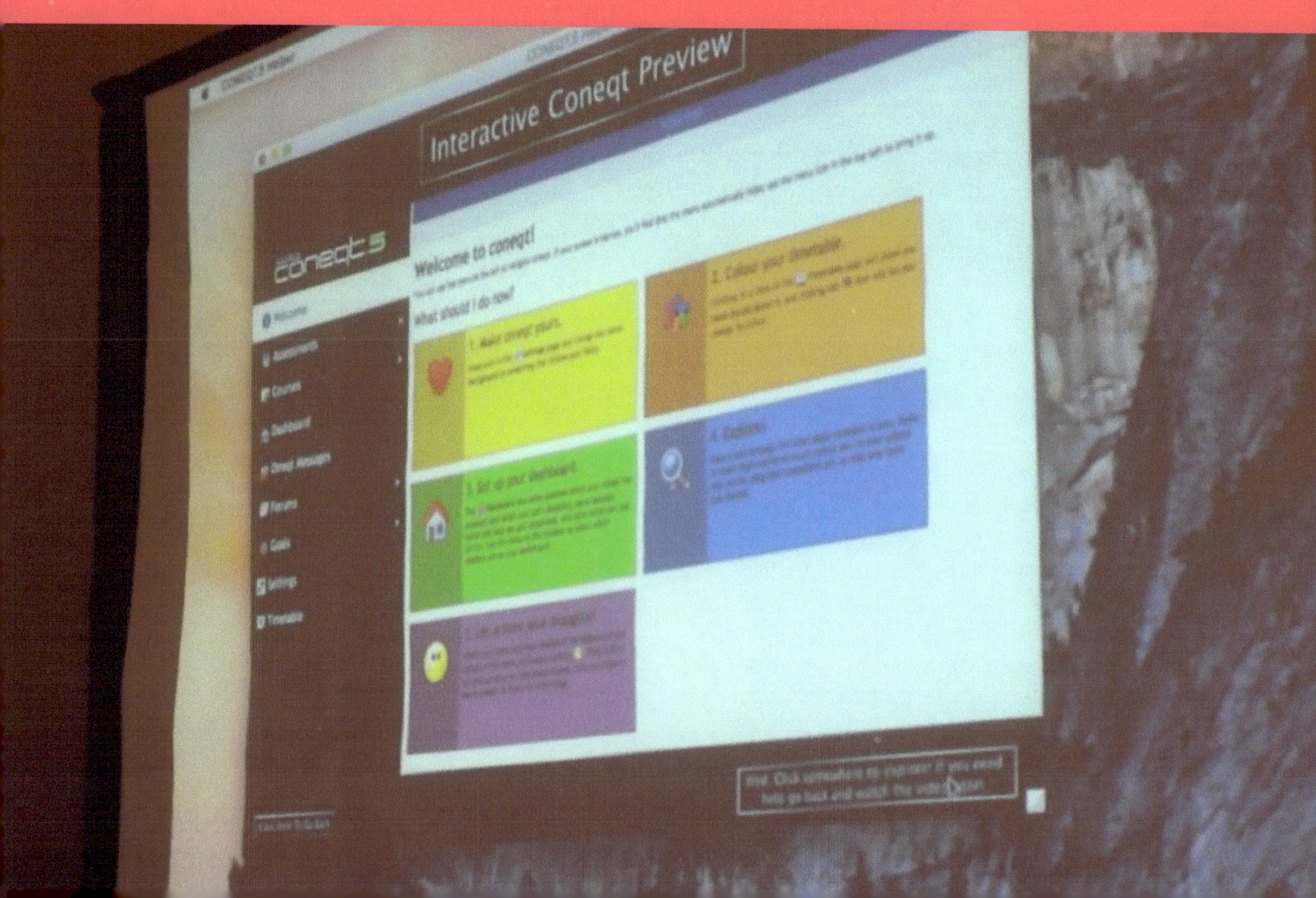

Building Bridges Between Important Content and Personal Meaning

A group of Year 7 students in Xavier College's Coding Club crowds around a laptop, engrossed in experimenting with CONEQT, the school's newly-installed student management system.

Ben: I wonder how it'll be like for everyone when we start using it? Will it take a lot of time to get used to? Is it going to be just a stressful experience?

Thomas: I suppose it'll work fine. Look, we've been trying it out and can navigate it easily.

Ben: But that's because we are in the Coding Club, right? What if a student is not? Will it be as easy? Especially if you are a new student. Imagine coming new to the school and having to use CONEQT to register for classes or to check your homework. That's a lot of added stress!

Thomas: Well…

Ben: New students will definitely have a harder time with it, I reckon. They'll have to get used to the school and classes and all, and on top of all that, get on the system quickly.

Matthias: Yeah, that could be a lot to deal with.

Ben: Maybe I can create something that can help…help them, like, get into it quickly.

Thomas: What do you mean? Like a training kind of thing?

Joshua: Like a workshop? Or set of instructions?

Ben: Maybe an app? Something that works like a workshop or has instructions to help them. I'll need to get into the backdoor of the system and see how it works. Maybe get some help to learn about this system and what I can do to make it more manageable.

¶ Xavier College is a Catholic school founded in 1878 by the Society of Jesus. It aims for excellence in education and the formation of reflective, compassionate, and articulate men and women of Christian faith, hope, and love who will provide outstanding service and leadership in the world.

> **Instead of the teacher teaching everything, it was more you think about what you need to learn, discuss that with your teacher, and he or she helps you to get the resources and the experts to learn it. So I kind of decided what my end goal was and how I was going to get there. That made it so much more interesting to me because there was personal value in what I was doing.**
> —Ben, student

What did using students' interests to drive their learning look like with older students, especially when achievement in placement examinations weighed heavily into the school's curricular choices? At Xavier College, Principal Chris Hayes encouraged teachers to always be on the lookout for opportunities to support student learning, particularly projects that would take them outside of the usual disciplines. For him, the questions to ask were: *How can we further engage and challenge each student? How can we as teachers give expression to the learning that matters? How can we inspire students to do more, to consider how things can be better, not only for the individual but for the community?*

When Year 7 student Ben became interested in creating an app to help students use the school's newly-installed student management system, CONEQT, more efficiently and effectively, his teacher Grant Butler saw an opportunity for engaging Ben's passion for solving problems encountered by his community and challenging him to push beyond the traditional school curriculum in order to come up with viable solutions.

Ben was a member of the school's Coding Club, which had grown out of the school's focus on taking into account each student's needs and interests and where they wanted to go in their learning. It had begun as an experiment to bring together students who were having difficulty making social connections in the school. When Grant realized that all the boys in the group had a common interest—computers—the Coding Club was born. For Chris, the initiative was worth supporting because it aligned with the school's vision of Xavier graduates: creative individuals with the passion to strive for excellence, the courage to serve others, and the confidence to pursue their dreams.

Ben's interest in improving the CONEQT user experience required him to learn a specific type of code—LifeCode—to enable him to create coded cards and buttons for a training module for users of the system. Grant and other computing teachers provided him with guidebooks on how to use the code, such as the kinds of variables, language, and programming logic for writing the appropriate code. Grant was also able to put Ben in touch with CONEQT's software developers, who gave him back-end access to CONEQT so that he could explore the system to figure out a way to meet the community's needs.

Being able to follow his own interest in learning gave Ben a new perspective on learning; he began to see the endeavor of learning as working towards something that was self-directed, authentic, useful, and meaningful:

> Instead of the teacher teaching everything, it was more you think about what you need to learn, discuss that with your teacher, and he or she helps you to get the resources and the experts to learn it. So I kind of decided what my end goal was and how I was going to get there. That made it so much more interesting to me because there was personal value in what I was doing. And I was doing something that would help other students.

The experience was especially rewarding for Ben because he "loved being able to fix a problem if there is one," and the opportunity to learn LifeCode gave him the confidence to go on to create other computer solutions to challenges faced by his school community.

How did Xavier College create the conditions for learning that were driven by student interests? How did teachers and leaders ensure that such conditions were sustained in the face of other competing commitments like examination success?

Xavier College believed in being responsive to student needs and creating institutionalized ways to support personalized learning when the opportunity arose. Chris recognized that leading the learning that mattered in the school often bumped up against state requirements in terms of the syllabus, particularly regarding the processes of evaluation and reporting. However, he saw the initiative to lead for the learning that mattered as an opportunity to emphasize the importance of creativity in learning because "when that becomes the focus, it forces us to deal with what education really is all about, to see that at the heart of it all, it's about the individual."

Chris's efforts to focus on the learning that mattered caused some tensions in the school, especially because the schooling day itself had become so busy. He understood that a worry for many on his staff

> …[It is critical to] use those tensions [created by the initiative to push toward the learning that matters] as creative tensions, and ask, *What is it that we are about in the school?* In fact, those tensions help to further define why we do what we do.
> — Chris Hayes, Principal

was how much time they were expected to devote to "the new thing." For him, it was even more critical then to "use those tensions as creative tensions, and ask, *What is it that we are about in the school?* In fact, those tensions help to further define why we do what we do." Chris recognized the importance of giving adequate time for the staff to reflect on and frame what they thought was the learning that mattered for their learners, given the school's vision, mission, and guiding principles. Chris saw learning opportunities like Ben's work on CONEQT as critical because they exemplified the school's commitment to each individual student's overall development.

Xavier College's encouragement of his interest in coding transformed Ben's outlook on life in the school. As an app developer, Ben was able to use his computer skills and passion for problem-solving to build strong relationships with his peers and teachers, thereby increasing his social connection to the community. He created a website that invited students and staff to reach out to him with their technological needs. In fact, when the school upgraded to a cashless system for students to pay for their tuckshop purchases with their student ID card, Ben brainstormed how students might top up their ID cards without their parents having to do it online using a credit card. For Ben, creating technological solutions to authentic problems had become his path towards Xavier's exhortation for students to "be a man for others," a man who reaches beyond school into the community and positions himself in service to others.

Part II
Navigating the Journey

Visions of the Learning that Matters

Leading Learning that Matters (LLtM) is an invitation to rethink what we teach. It's an invitation to focus on learning that matters. Of course, *how* we teach—text and discussion, project-based learning, in person or online, etc.—has to be considered, but first and foremost LLtM explores *what* we teach.

Learning that matters is an aspirational concept. It's what we are reaching for. It's learning that speaks powerfully to learners' lives going forward, learning that helps inform and energize their personal lives, their civic lives, their aesthetic lives, their religious lives, and just about any other aspect of their experience.

Of course, any educational institution aims in this general direction. The mission and vision of LLtM is to intensify and deepen this focus, looking toward schools that serve even more powerfully the futures of their students and society generally. This section focuses on learning that matters, while the next section focuses on the leadership process.

Learning that matters—that phrase raises many questions. Why does learning that matters invite attention? What does learning that matters look like? What does *learning that matters* actually mean, beyond a nice sounding phrase? How might the faculty of a school go about such a quest? We'll make a start on such questions in this section and deepen the story throughout the rest of this book.

Why does learning that matters invite attention?

Any school cares about learning that matters in a broad sense. This is what schools are for! As educators, we all strive to cultivate skills, understandings, and commitments that will figure frequently and significantly in students' lives. We're teaching toward thoughtful and energetic citizens. We're teaching toward good collaborators. We're nourishing ethical commitments. We'd like to foster adults who can engage the arts meaningfully and rewardingly, relate to family members and others well, and contribute to various professions with energy and intelligence.

The question is not so much whether learning that matters is on the radar as whether we could be doing more . . . even much more.

The challenge today reflects the complex history of education across decades and centuries. Over time, school practices and traditional curricula have developed expectations about what's important, about what learning goes with various disciplines, about what topics need to get covered, and so on. Some standard topics are clear contributions to learning that matters. But too often, a standard topic X is "there because it is there." It's just part of the canon.

For a provocative example, consider a contrast between two mathematics topics: quadratic equations, and statistics and probability. Most students study quadratic equations at some point, but hardly any student ever uses quadratic equations later in life, unless that student enters a technical career.

Whether students study statistics and probability varies across schools and nations. Often students do not do so very deeply. However, statistics and probability, particularly in their basics, come up all the time in areas like personal medical decisions, insurance decisions, gambling, understanding public policies, and much more. Statistics and probability are high-payoff topics!

So why are quadratic equations so often prioritized over statistics and probability? To a considerable extent, because quadratic equations are "there because they are there." Quadratic equations are part of the canon rather than a considered choice with genuine utility in mind.

Similar examples can be sketched in virtually any discipline. There are always corners of the discipline that are part of the canon but really don't deliver much for most learners later in life. Then there are other corners of the same discipline that deliver a lot, and would deliver even more if they were taught with greater breadth and depth.

But let's pause for a moment. Let's not be too categorical. Is our example an argument against teaching quadratic equations? Perhaps I'm a mathematics teacher and I love to teach quadratic equations. I can teach it in ways that genuinely interest my students, and I think it's something that students should know and understand and appreciate. Also, I have to consider the style and commitments of the institution.

All true! Quadratic equations versus statistics and probability is just an example. It's an example that makes sense in many settings but not in all. Perhaps in your context, in your school, quadratic equations is one of the perfect topics.

The point of LLtM is not to dictate what counts as "mattering." The point, rather, is to provoke and support a deep conversation that considers how the content we teach today will play out for our students over time, particularly in students' lives beyond school. In most schools, the conversation simply has not occurred in a broad collaborative way. Let's have the conversation!

What does learning that matters look like?

Schools that have had the conversation about learning that matters naturally and appropriately move in somewhat different directions . . . but not completely different directions, because any school shares a need to prepare learners meaningfully for their roles in today's world. One of the best ways to get a feel for the kinds of teaching and learning that emerge is to look to some examples. Let's consider a few cases from schools that have participated in LLtM, including a few that are detailed in Part I, *Pictures of Practice*. At Overnewton Anglican Community College, the Year 5 unit on 19th century colonial Australia was revised so that students learned about and understood different perspectives on migration and connected their learning to the refugee crisis in the world today. As the students delved into 19th century colonial Australia, they explored the significance of migration in the past as well as in our contemporary society. They considered the wider and multifaceted implications of migration well beyond typical textbook applications: *How do different people experience migration? What are the multiple push and pull factors for migrating, and how has migration impacted origin countries and receiving communities? Who are the refugees, and why should we care about them?*

In Ivanhoe Girls' Grammar School, the Year 12 literature curriculum supported students in building bridges between the disciplinary content in the literature syllabus and the students' interests and commitments. In literature lessons, students grappled with their emerging ideas and questions; articulated and interrogated their theories about themselves, their community, and the world; and examined their own lived experiences. Texts such as Henrik Ibsen's *A Doll's House* and Jane Austen's *Pride and Prejudice* offered rich contexts for them to explore the role of women in traditional and male-dominated societies, and to make sense of social mores—ambition, expectations, marriage, class, taboos—both in the era of the texts and in 21st century Australia and the world.

At Beaconhills College, Year 5 students figured out how much money it would take to build a well for an African community and how they could raise the money for it. What started as a science lesson looking at the *how* and *why* of recycling took on a momentum that drew in other disciplines as students began to wrap their minds around the reality that there were adults and children dying in the world because they had no access to clean drinking water.

Instead of coming into the classroom to "do" mathematics or science or language arts or religion, the students took an interdisciplinary approach to formulating feasible solutions. They researched the causes and impact of water-borne diseases and investigated why particular communities were more at risk than others (*science*); calculated how many cans they needed to recycle to raise the sum required (*mathematics*); and reached out to the larger school community using informative posters to explain their cause, giving short speeches in different classrooms to emphasize why their cause mattered and writing emails to parents that made it clear why they were embarking on the project (*language arts*).

What characterizes learning that matters?

There is a rule-of-thumb answer to this question that applies to any setting. And there's a particular side that reflects the institution in question. The general rule-of-thumb answer is: we want learning that lasts and makes a difference in students' lives. As educators, we're in it for the long game. We want learning not just for the test or the essay at the end of the unit. We want learning that surfaces later with some frequency in students' lives, informing and energizing how they engage the world. If some part of what we're teaching doesn't seem likely to do that, maybe we shouldn't be teaching so much of that part. If some part of what we're teaching *does* offer high payoff in the long term, maybe we should be teaching it in a deeper, wider way.

But there's more to this than the general rule-of-thumb about high payoff in the long term. LLtM embraces the idea that schools are different. Schools have distinctive histories, commitments, and aspirations. Some goals in the foreground at one institution may be in the background at another.

For instance, some schools have characteristic religious commitments. Part of the mission is to advance students' understanding of and engagement with a faith. Some schools foreground a disciplinary area, for instance science-oriented schools preparing students for participation in mathematics and the sciences. Some schools foreground the arts. Some pay extensive attention to social responsibility. And, of course, many schools adopt a mix of themes.

From the standpoint of learning that matters, these differences are something to celebrate. Neither students nor society would be well-served if every educational institution did the same thing! Also, in a somewhat competitive environment, it makes good sense to consider how a school is positioned in the "marketplace" of education—what's on offer that's special and especially forward-looking in our complex globalized world.

In summary, LLtM is an invitation to think hard in a general way about how what's learned might go forward in learners' lives, and to think hard about the particular institution and what its character means for the learning that matters.

How do schools reach toward visions of learning that matters?

Conversation is the name of the game. Schools pursue learning that matters through collective efforts—webs of conversation, ideas listed on whiteboards, stickies posted on walls, categories organized and reorganized, informal debates, reviews of the school history, touching base with the school board or parents. The endeavor looks beyond individual faculty members towards something more communitarian. Faculty members formulate a broad vision of the kind of learning that matters in their institution. Individual and departmental choices occur within the context of that broad vision. Typically, the vision is roomy rather than narrow, generous rather than strict, but it does set a direction that expresses the spirit of the institution and builds coherence.

None of this means that every faculty member participates fully from the beginning. Naturally some are more interested at first. Some members of the faculty may never be all that interested. However, overall the initiative has an emphatically community spirit.

A case in point is Woodleigh School's Penbank Campus, where the vision for the learning that matters is collectively crafted and consistently refined by all the teachers at staff meetings. Teachers are regularly invited to take stock of that vision: *Let's look back on the dreams that we had previously framed for our students. How do we feel about them now? What do we feel is the learning that really matters to us now?* Curriculum planning meetings are likewise collaborative, and everyone is free to bring up ideas and raise questions. Curriculum leaders work on the premise that their role is to get discussions going, so that teachers own their ideas and their learning, getting engaged in the collective enterprise of designing the learning that matters for their students.

At Ivanhoe Girls' Grammar School, a team of curriculum leaders is convened across different disciplinary areas, bringing them into conversation with one another, in the process enriching and broadening how they think about the learning that matters. The curriculum leaders come to understand how all the different parts of the school work together towards the larger enterprise of preparing their students for the contemporary world. They collaborate across disciplinary aisles to design learning experiences that nurture their students toward their overall vision of the learning that matters: confident, courageous, and critical thinkers who are generous of spirit, have a lifelong love of learning, and use their voices to create positive change.

Tools for exploring ideas for learning that matters

Rethinking what learning truly matters for our students goes better with the help of some tools. In this book, you'll find a collection of tools for the purpose. Let's preview. One tool identifies six "Beyonds" of education (see page 71 in Part III, *Tools and Tips*, for details). It's a diagram defining six directions of

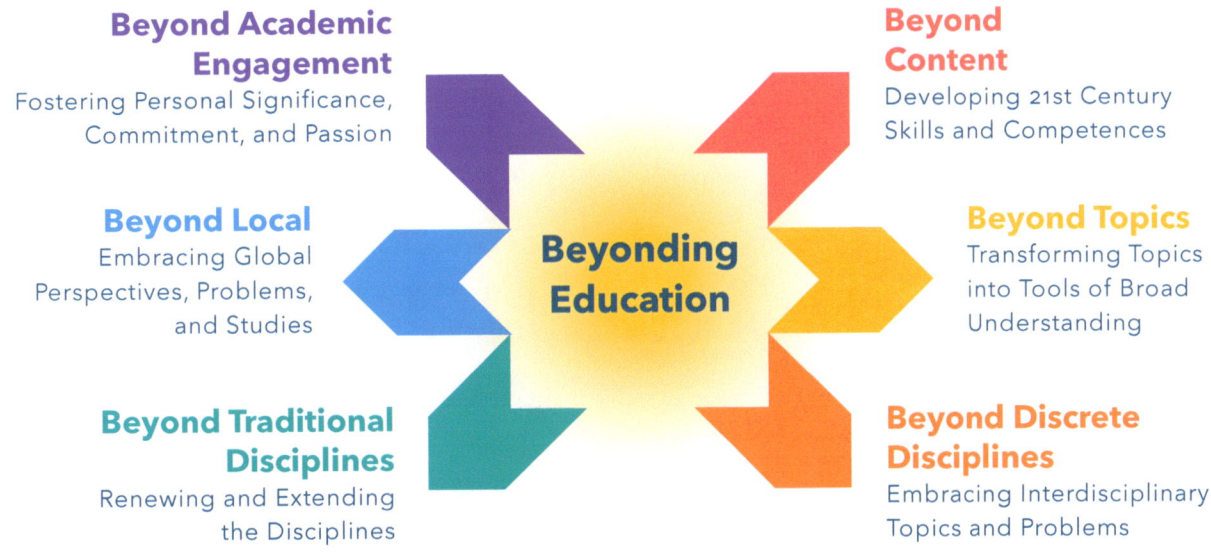

innovation prominent around the world in various schools and government frameworks. The categories emerged from informal surveys.

The Six Beyonds provide one structure within which to brainstorm ideas for learning that matters. Individual teachers and groups of teachers in conversation can ask, *What are we doing now? Where might we want to push further? Which Beyonds are most natural to our commitments and aspirations?* Let's consider two examples and how they relate to the Beyonds.

To broaden the impact of service learning at Good Shepherd Lutheran Primary School, Principal Greg Schneider began exploring how the time-honored tradition of service learning might be "beyonded": *How can the experience of fundraising for a Cambodian community be made more authentic and relevant for our students? How can we help students move beyond simple conceptions of the receiving community as poor and deprived, and come to understand deeply the complex history and culture of the Cambodian people?*

Greg envisioned two major shifts: refocusing from raising funds to raising awareness about the welfare of others, and reframing the program from a series of extracurricular activities to thoughtfully sequenced learning experiences within and across the disciplines. His vision shifted the conversation from *We serve because we have more* to *We serve because we are part of a global humanity*, and prepared students to engage with a global problem—poverty—by considering its myriad causes through multiple disciplinary lenses.

It also challenged students to grapple with conflicting positions—*What kind of aid/service is more effective? More ethical? More sustainable? For whom?*—that even experts struggle with. Perhaps most importantly, the shift invited the students to examine their own identity and relationship to the world in the act of service—*Who am I and why do I serve?* Grounding lessons in politics, geography, and economics supported the students in understanding why and how the Cambodian food supply and forest reserves are imperiled. Investigating the history and politics of aid for Cambodia sparked discussion about what impact external aid has had on Cambodia and its people, as well as how the notion of "aid" has shaped the way Cambodians and citizens of the giving countries view the other and themselves.

Looking back at the Six Beyonds, this example reaches beyond local to global perspectives, beyond discrete disciplines to interdisciplinary perspectives, and beyond a somewhat academic fund-raising exercise to dimensions of understanding with more personal overtones.

Another example comes from Xavier College, where art teachers foregrounded contemporary art practice by inviting Year 12 students to create meaningful art in public spaces. Instead of fashioning and exhibiting individual artwork in formal studio and gallery spaces, students created art that was community-driven, community-inspired, and inclusive. Tasked with making visible the school's guiding themes of "Setting Hearts on Fire" and "A Faith that Does Justice" in the main school courtyard, the students decided to invite the views of their peers and integrate those views into the design so that the courtyard would become a shared space expressing diverse ideas. The final design was a collaborative and complex set of images on tiles that represented the myriad views of more than one hundred Year 12 students. It was literally, in the words of one student, "everyone putting their ideas and passion into the school."

From the conceptualization of images and colors to the actual painting and mounting of the mosaic tiles, the students mirrored the practice of many contemporary artists, whose work responds to the globally influenced and culturally diverse world and gives voice to the varied and changing cultural landscape of identity, values, and beliefs. The transformation of the courtyard was, in essence, a junior version of expert artistic practice, an integration of the multiple voices of the student community into a coherent design that articulated the complex identity of the Xavier seniors.

Looking back at the Six Beyonds, this example reaches beyond content to some 21st century skills, beyond the traditional disciplines to renewals and extensions, and beyond academic engagement to personally significant engagement with the school as a community.

In Part III of this book, you'll find other tools besides the Beyonds for envisioning the learning that matters. Some of those tools, including the Beyonds, guide creative exploration of possibilities:

Beyonding Education, *which we just looked at.*

Mattermatics. *This playful brainstorming tool invites educators to formulate one topic they do not teach now that they might add (+1); one topic they do teach now that they might expand (x 2); and one topic they teach now that they might shrink to make room (÷ 3).*

Expanding Topics to Matter More. *This tool offers several ideas for taking a topic already being taught and expanding it to matter more.*

Some tools offer critical assessments of promising themes and topics, to be sure they really matter to the lives students live:

Opportunity Story. *This involves telling a story to ourselves about how a candidate theme or topic might play out in the long term for learners, especially beyond their academic program.*

Accept No Substitutes. *This tool offers a checklist of important criteria for good learning, such as deep learning and rigor, that we want to honor, but that don't necessarily go as far as learning that matters. Experience shows that sometimes these are taken as complete substitutes for learning that matters. We want them…but we want more!*

While building this new road, what happens to the familiar road?

In the fantasy version of LLtM, school faculty members get together in various groups and subgroups toward the end of one academic year. They sort it all out. At the beginning of the next academic year, the school launches a new world of learning, one that matters as never before.

Yes, it's a fantasy! Experience with LLtM says that serious time is needed to stand back, rethink, and create a vision. People are always busy. Out of the gate, some are more concerned or interested than others, although energy builds over time. Moreover, the new vision doesn't just get figured out and installed. It continues to evolve, sometimes substantially. Change is substantive but incremental. Meanwhile, most of the familiar road of established and effective teaching/learning processes needs to keep operating.

Schools involved in LLtM strike a balance between exploring new possibilities for learning that matters and keeping established agendas in motion. LLtM is woven into the very important ongoing commitment of the institution to support student learning effectively day by day, week by week.

And here's a further question: *Should we expect to change everything, even if not in the short term?*

No, of course not. The new road overlaps the familiar road a lot! In any school, many themes and topics already contribute to learning that matters. Maybe those themes and topics can be placed more in the foreground. Maybe they can be taught a little more deeply or a little more broadly for more transfer of learning. But you can be sure they are there!

Furthermore, there will always be some themes and topics that have to be taught, at least in an abbreviated form and sometimes in full form, even though they may not fully meet the school's own aspirations for learning that matters. Why? Because they are on the national exams, because they are part of university expectations for students who hope to go on to university, because they figure in state mandates.

Usually such themes and topics can be explored with students in somewhat broader ways, ways that at least reach toward a richer conception of learning that matters. But for some topics, maybe not even that. No worries! The important challenge is *not* to make every moment of every day a learning that matters epiphany. Rather, the important challenge is to increase learning that matters substantially.

To recall a familiar mantra, "The best is the enemy of the good." If we insist on pure, ideal learning that matters every hour of the school day, we will almost certainly fail. If we reach energetically and persistently for much more presence of learning that truly matters, we will almost certainly succeed.

Four Leadership Practices

School leaders that take the learning that matters journey follow similar paths to those illustrated in Part I, *Pictures of Practice*. They orchestrate conversations with teachers over time about what learning that matters looks like in their setting. They listen to students and their community to understand what knowledge and skills will matter most for lives students are likely to live. Leaders create opportunities for teachers to examine existing curricular choices and promote experimentation. By focusing on the learning that matters (*what is worth learning*), they open up possibilities beyond more traditional conversations about methods of teaching (*how it will be learned*) and evaluation (*how to know that learning has happened*).

Questions about instruction and assessment are important, particularly today when schools are increasingly considering online and distance learning technologies. However, too often questions of teaching methods and evaluation narrow a school's focus, leading to incremental solutions that do not address deeper problems of education. Schools may get better at delivery and assessment, but not face the more fundamental challenge of remaining relevant to their learners and their communities in a swiftly changing world.

Transforming the content of learning is at the heart of a school's LLtM journey. It is a complex challenge for schools as they attempt to adapt to the demands of contemporary society. National standards, assessments, and curricula can often be experienced as restrictive forces in schools, offering prefabricated answers to, and placing external limits on, what learning matters. The Six Beyonds introduced on page 43 are levers for systematically transforming typical content for greater depth, reach, and significance. The Beyonds are examples of how schools are opening up ways to engage teachers, students, and others in relevant content.

Leadership as a complex ecology of influences

Even amidst today's rapidly changing landscape, it is worth noting that not all challenges that schools and leaders face are complex. There are many everyday technical problems leaders can solve by giving their staff clear answers and direction, pointing them to established strategies to put into place. However, what learning matters is not such a simple question with technical solutions. It is complex because of our complex world. It calls into question *for whom* and *why?* Answers emerge, creating new knowledge through problem finding, experimentation, and developing new practices.

The journey of answering such a challenging question is not a path to be travelled alone. It encourages leaders to adopt a more distributed notion of leadership: leadership as the process of engaging the social network in co-creating ideas and directions. This engagement can look different depending on your school's needs and structure.

For example, supporting staff to implement the learning that matters in Overnewton Anglican Community College required coherence and alignment across the school. Principal Jim Laussen and his leadership team of eighteen realized this would be a challenge. To assist the leadership team to be more effective, Jim reorganized it into two teams, one for operational issues (e.g., policy, finances, management, etc.) and the other for purely academic matters. Next, he created a cascading system of instructional leadership in which he met regularly with the heads of the lower, middle, and upper schools to discuss what learning matters and share progress and needs. After each meeting, the heads brought ideas back to their teaching and learning committees who, in turn, worked closely with teachers to reimagine the learning in the classroom.

For Executive Principal Jill Healey at Flinders Christian Community College, the first step toward engaging her network in the learning that matters was to construct a big picture of what success looked like. With a clear destination in mind, Jill worked with her teams of curriculum leaders and teachers to identify the key steps towards the goal of reimagining content for the school. The teams then worked collaboratively to determine priorities and plan feasible, often bite-sized, projects that were critical steps towards the overall vision.

At Beaconhills College, Headmaster Tony Sheumack used the concept of learning that matters as a lens to help his leadership team arrive at what eventually became their "six pillars of learning and holistic education." These pillars now guide curricular innovation and review in the school. Getting to a simple and elegant statement of the learning that matters took the team two years. That might sound like a long time, but the two years were well spent because they allowed the team to consult with the staff to test and refine the vision. Consequently, the school's current integrated curriculum, which stemmed from the collective thinking about what learning matters, enjoyed school-wide support because it was intentionally designed so everyone felt ownership of it.

As these illustrate, leadership happens throughout a school. It is not just what the leader does; rather, leadership in these schools is the social process of setting direction and influencing thinking and behaviors toward shared educational goals. The social influences that impact student learning come from an ecology of sources, including teachers, principals, school and classroom conditions, and families.

In order to explore the question of what learning matters, we need a way to understand who to involve and what influences the quality of learning at the school. The Ecology of Social Influences tool is one way for LLtM leaders to begin to explore these questions (see Part III for more on this tool). It asks leaders to locate the learning that matters

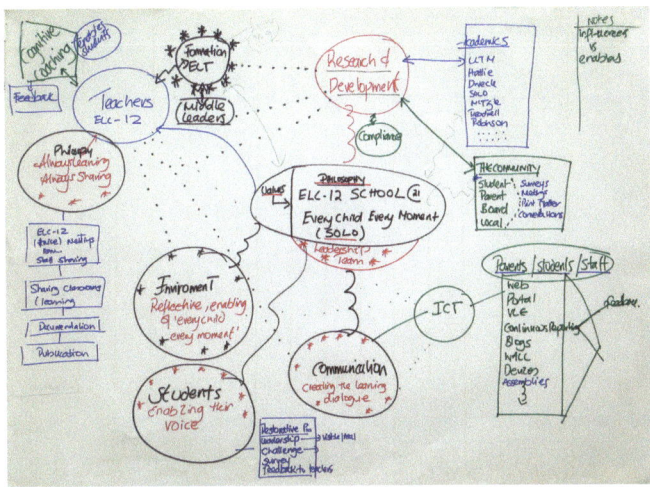

at the heart, then brainstorm how various stakeholders and forces shape the thinking and practices toward that goal.

The example above shows the influences mapped by Westbourne Grammar School Principal Meg Hansen early in her LLtM journey. When Meg and the other LLtM principals shared and discussed their maps, they were surprised by how their colleagues mapped the influences, as well as encouraged by the many connections they saw across the maps, such as the powerful role that student voice had in shaping the learning that matters. Meg reflected:

> It's surprising where the influence comes from. …Many of our colleagues might be thinking that influence comes from the structure and the person who's got the title….What we're starting to find is that students can and should have enormous influence on learning as long as we enable their voice. It was an unexpected influence, but it was so important.

Four key practices of LLtM

To lead learning that matters, leaders like Meg, Tony, Jim, and Jill make choices about how to best engage others—students, teachers, and community members—in the process. Over several years of documenting the journeys of LLtM principals, we have identified four essential practices of leaders that support a school's focus on the learning that matters: *creating shared vision, developing collaborative structures, supporting individual development,* and *sustaining progress.*

Creating shared vision

This practice speaks to the way in which a leader becomes a change agent for a system by involving a variety of stakeholders in shaping a compelling and shared vision of learning that matters in their community. These leaders allow answers to emerge over time. Tools such as Ecology of Social Influences and Voices to Vision are strategies to help leaders fuel and focus on this practice. What follows are some lessons from LLtM principals on how to frame the invitation, who to include, and how the vision should be shared and created:

- *Create a simple, clear, compelling invitation to others*
- *Connect the vision to the school's strategic direction, identity, and philosophy*
- *Focus on the future, but learn from the school's past*
- *Engage the voices of teachers, students, and other stakeholders*
- *Promote a shared moral purpose across stakeholders*
- *Set expectations that the vision should change over time*
- *Have clear roles and expectations so the community understands how people are working together*
- *Challenge the status quo and assumptions about what learning matters*
- *Don't be afraid to change and model the willingness to change*
- *Once the vision takes shape, communicate it often to everyone*
- *Share the vision in a variety of ways and make it visible for everyone in the school*
- *Share stories of what the vision looks like*
- *Encourage others to own the vision and communicate it in their own words*
- *Create long-term and short-term goals that connect to the vision*
- *Don't try to do too much; you may need to cut other initiatives or distractions*

Developing collaborative structures

To lead for the learning that matters, principals develop a variety of structures to support the interdependent learning and experimentation needed among stakeholders. These structures create spaces to think together, as well as processes to share ideas, encourage risk-taking, and learn from mistakes and feedback. Their focus is often on redesigning how faculty meetings happen, how voices of stakeholders are involved in decisions, and how physical spaces themselves can aid in collaboration. The Documenting Learning that Matters and the Learning Frame and Windows tools are offered as supports for the practice. Some insights on this practice from LLtM principals include:

- *Break down silos by creating teams and inquiry groups across all staff*
- *Delegate, engage, and empower teams to create experiments, goals, and plans*
- *In faculty meetings, look for roles that are missing and fill them*
- *Give staff time and permission to share divergent*

opinions
- Design meeting spaces to support ideation: whiteboards, sticky notes, etc.
- Honor experiments and risk-taking
- Celebrate successes in teacher meetings (and also laugh and learn from missteps)
- Create traditions in meetings that share what learning that matters looks like
- Allow teachers to share and make their progress visible
- Give teachers tools to offer one another feedback on their experiments
- Keep the change and progress visible in all meetings
- Invite parents and community to offer external feedback
- Ensure you have the right people in the right places
- Listen and adapt to community concerns

Supporting individual development

When leaders support the individual development of their teachers, staff, and stakeholders, they create stimulating conditions for them to develop capacities for learning and change. This involves tapping into their intrinsic motivation and beliefs to support a shift towards the learning that matters. It develops agency so that the teachers, staff, and stakeholders are able to experiment and take risks with one another. Insights from LLtM principals include understanding the variety of needs, the challenges that may emerge, and the ways to spark the learning within a community:

- Know your teacher and staff needs, beliefs, and motivations at all levels
- Look for excitement and champions early
- Expect resistance; respond with courage and clarity
- Don't worry about laggards, but know what will make it worthwhile for them
- Invite individuals to identify goals for change and growth
- Create inspiration among teachers; encourage sharing stories
- Use research and outsiders to stimulate ideas and provoke conversations
- Engender well-being for all involved—real change is hard work
- Create coaching and mentoring relationships among staff
- Recruit, hire, and onboard staff with the learning that matters vision in mind
- Develop succession plans for all positions with the vision in mind
- Be kind, supportive, and encouraging when missteps happen
- Focus on developing empowerment and self-authorship at all levels
- Respect the progress and emphasize accountability to one another

Sustaining progress

Embedding the processes for the learning that matters into the everyday work of a school is the cornerstone of this practice. Often, as things roll along in an initiative and the general feeling is that it is all going well, people never get to thinking about institutionalization, making the initiative fragile. Sustaining the learning that matters in a school involves allocating time and other resources to support teachers; it can also mean protecting teachers from distractions. Principals on the LLtM journey find the right moments to push teachers but wisely recognize when not to. Sustaining progress also means preparing to defend the initiative against natural skeptics as well as taking steps to institutionalize LLtM in the fabric of school policies and systems. Insights from LLtM principals include:

- *Don't jump too quickly; be patient but persistent*
- *Go slow and steady (fads will fade)*
- *Control the sprawl; maintain focus; don't get distracted*
- *Regularly read the mood of staff and stakeholders throughout the process*
- *Monitor the appetite for and pace of change*
- *Anticipate arguments against change; be ready to defend the vision*
- *Look for ways to embed processes into meetings, agendas, planning, evaluations, etc.*
- *Find smart ways to institutionalize LLtM into planning, hiring, and reporting systems*
- *Develop frameworks and language that support the learning that matters*
- *Use shared, inclusive language as a way to help change practice*
- *Look for simple systems that can support the change*
- *Create weekly reflection and learning time; protect it from other demands*

Of course, these four practices—creating shared vision, developing collaborative structures, supporting individual development, and sustaining progress—are by no means the only leadership moves that effective leaders employ in shepherding change in their school contexts. In working with LLtM schools, though, we have found that the enterprise of transforming the content of learning to meet the demands of contemporary society invariably requires that leaders pay attention to these four practices.

The First Months

The first months of Leading Learning that Matters are in many ways the most exciting, the most intriguing, the most energizing. They are also the most challenging. There's so much to be decided: *Who will be involved? Who will play early roles as others engage later? What approach to learning that matters expresses the school's history, commitments, and aspirations?* Emerging answers to these questions will continue to shape the trajectory of LLtM in a school for years to come.

Here we offer a broad sketch of the first months. We're also trying to avoid pat formulas. After all, every setting is different. The schools that have already participated in LLtM reveal individual circumstances of pace and direction. Many scenarios can work and the only universal mantra is: Let's get going!

What does it look like to finish those first months?

The first months are not a precise period of time or a precise measure of progress. Even so, one can ask in a rough and ready sense what a good start looks like. Some help comes from the four practices discussed in the previous section: *creating shared vision, developing collaborative structures, supporting individual development,* and *sustaining progress.* Let's consider them one by one.

Creating shared vision

As the first months round out, the school leadership and participating staff can say what the relevant history and commitments and aspirations of their institution look toward—a foundation for global citizenship, grounding in a particular religion and its moral commitments, preparation for a career in math and science, development of strong self-awareness and self-management as a learner, or any of many other possibilities. A glance back at the Six Beyonds introduced on page 43 or a look ahead to Part III for learning that matters tools can provide some particulars to advance this conversation.

The emerging shared vision expresses the core commitment of learning that matters—content and skills and approaches to teaching/learning that will genuinely continue to matter in the lives of students as they grow and develop, in ways meaningful in society, beyond the immediate and sometimes overly-focused demands of conventional curricula.

For example, Woodleigh School's Penbank Campus focuses on investigation and inquiry as an integral part of the curriculum (see Part I, *Pictures of Practice,* for more on this example and others below). The focus highlights its commitment to nurturing students who are architects of their own learning, a core competency that the staff agrees is key to success in contemporary society. The school's learning centers engage the students' curiosity and interests, reflecting the way the teachers carefully and deliberately create rich opportunities for students to personalize and pursue their own learning.

Developing collaborative structures

As the first months round out, a look around a school reveals several structures supporting the LLtM process. These might include, for example, regular check-ins on LLtM progress at staff meetings and check-ins during department meetings. They might include leadership roles for individuals who have signaled special interest and wish to champion particular initiatives toward the learning that matters. These roles might involve general planning or working with groups of faculty.

Collaborative structures might include special interest groups of staff that meet now and again, for instance, those from different departments interested in fostering global awareness or nurturing student autonomy and self-management. Groups that cut across typical divisions and roles can help to build a community beyond organizational silos.

At The Good Shepherd Lutheran Primary School, Principal Greg Schneider invited his staff to explore collectively how they might best prepare their students for our contemporary world. The staff wrote their individual ideas on stickies and then together categorized them on charts. These are displayed prominently in the teachers' room. The staff is encouraged to review the charts continually and debate their ideas, in the process building a strong sense of ownership over the vision of the learning that matters in the school. This collaborative process opened the door for teachers to work together to transform what and how they teach in the classroom, moving them away from operating in silos, towards connecting what they do in the classroom to the larger vision for learning in the school.

Supporting individual development

As the first months round out, staff members have received encouragement to contribute to the process of crafting a vision of learning that matters for the school and to explore possible directions in their own teaching resonant with this vision. *Is there a new course I might teach? A favorite topic that already expresses the vision that I might expand?* Staff members have been given license and support to try experiments, to collaborate, to gather and reflect on how things are going and what puzzles are emerging. The process has kindled in many a new opportunity to pursue their beliefs about what's most important, tapping staff members' intrinsic motivation.

For instance, at Beaconhills College, Headmaster Tony Sheumack and his leadership team encourage staff to suggest and collaborate on innovative projects that contribute to nurturing confident and independent learners who understand their responsibility to care for their community. These "champions," as Tony describes them, are encouraged to innovate within what they are already doing, instead of reaching for expansive, large-scale change that may not be sustainable. Teacher Lynette George proposed bringing together traditions from the Christian faith and the Indigenous community in a sacred circle setting constructed within the school.

With the encouragement and support of the leadership team, Lynette now runs a program for students to spend time reflecting alone or with a group in the sacred circle. The program aligns well with the school's vision of nurturing students' capacity to appreciate thoughtful discussion and quiet reflection as powerful practices in both the Christian and Indigenous traditions, as well as in contemporary living and learning.

Sustaining progress

As the first months round out, the school leadership has taken steps to share the initiative in the community—with not only staff but also students, the school board, and parents. The leadership has found ways to assure stakeholders that the initiative includes a strong commitment to the identity of the school. The leadership may have found ways to rein in or postpone other initiatives a bit, since often school settings are cluttered with too many uncoordinated initiatives at the same time. LLtM is pursued in the spirit of innovation, preparing students for our complex contemporary world without diminishing, indeed building on, what the institution already does well.

This process of sharing goes beyond terse information. Advice has been sought. Vivid examples have been shared. For instance, Principal Meg Hansen of Westbourne Grammar School regularly communicates the school's initiatives to the staff and parents, recruiting them as partners in the school's endeavor to nurture thoughtful, reflective, and resilient learners. Every staff meeting, whether for curriculum leaders, year-level teams, or the whole staff, focuses squarely on learning: *How are curricular innovations working out? What are some ways that the programs could be improved? What are some obstacles that should be surfaced and worked through?*

To make visible to parents how their children are experiencing school, Meg holds regular parent information evenings. She has also launched a parents' portal where parents can browse the academic materials that the teachers and leadership have been reading to inform their curricular plans and decisions, watch recordings of parent information meetings, submit questions they may have, and familiarize themselves with the entire curricular scope and forms of assessment used in the classes.

Those then are some of the earmarks signaling the very approximate end of the first months.

We've mentioned before that participants in LLtM may be part of a cohort of several schools and principals. This was the case with the original group. It might seem a little challenging to stand back from these earmarks and take stock, so if you are part of a cohort, this can help. The principals in the original cohort emphasized again and again how effective it was to talk things over with colleagues going through the same process in their own institutions. The power of conversation contributes not only within but across schools. (For more on the cohort model, see the next section, *On the Journey Together*.)

How long are those "first months"?

Although the period of the "first months" lacks sharp definition, experience lets us estimate a rough range: four to eight months during an academic year, with six months a good middle ground. Certainly momentum can be established in less than four months. It would be really impressive, though, if that momentum had accomplished a good start on all four practices—creating shared vision, developing collaborative structures, supporting individual development, and sustaining progress. In fact, the first months have often emphasized the staff collaboratively envisioning what learning matters for their students and identifying opportunities for such learning. At The Good Shepherd Lutheran Primary School, Principal Greg Schneider and his leadership team set aside time for the staff to articulate an initial vision of the learning that matters and created opportunities for them to continue to refine it. Greg describes how a clear vision was especially critical, providing his staff and him with a sharper lens for curricular decisions and greater discernment about the support needed to encourage innovation towards that vision. If eight months seem clearly short of a good start, some head scratching is in order. After all, eight months approaches a typical school year. Such a situation might mean that other circumstances having nothing to do with LLtM have disrupted the initiative. Or it might mean that in some broad sense the institution is not ready for LLtM. Certainly the situation invites some pondering over the causes of a somewhat slow process and considering what to do next.

This is a good opportunity to slip in another orienting question about the timeline. If the first months usually range from four to eight, how long does the entire LLtM process require? Again there is no crisp answer, but around two years seem needed for an LLtM initiative to settle into a steady rhythm in an educational setting. In some cases, three.

But wait—in no sense is LLtM "done" at that point. After two years of Leading Learning that Matters in his school, Greg Schneider concluded, "We still have a long way to go . . . and the further we proceed, the more questions we ask ourselves." Pursuing learning that matters is not like constructing a building, installing the furniture, moving in, and that's that. It's a continuing process that becomes part of the culture of the institution.

Here again let's remember the experience of principals functioning in a cohort. Some schools move ahead more quickly, some less so. Having a mix of cases in the conversation, when that's possible, certainly aids in calibrating progress and calculating next steps.

What are some specific and important actions during those first months?

If a school can get started well on the four practices—shared vision, collaborative structures, individual development, and sustained progress—how to advance further becomes much clearer. A context has been established. Next steps almost suggest themselves. So what are "first steps" that lead up to those "next steps"? For help on this, you will find on the following pages the First Months Launch List, which assembles a number of actions school leaders have found helpful during the first months in advancing LLtM. The First Months Launch List can be a useful tool in planning and tracking progress.

That said, it is important to approach the First Months Launch List in a flexible spirit. Read it over. See how it seems to flow. Compose a rough plan that makes sense in your context. Look back at the First Months Launch List occasionally, judging what can be checked off, what needs attention, and what doesn't fit your context. A few particulars:

- *Not everything has to get checked off! These are tips, not a formula.*
- *Undoubtedly there will be other matters you'll want to address. Not everything that needs attention is going to be on the First Months Launch List.*
- *The order of the First Months Launch List reflects only an approximate sequence. Certainly some steps could be taken earlier or later.*

The First Months Launch List is definitely not a march, one by one, through the four practices of shared vision, collaborative structures, individual development, and sustained progress. However, there is a rough order. The early focus falls on shared vision, while soon collaborative structures come into the picture, and then individual development, with some attention toward the end of the launch list to sustained progress. A tag appears at the end of each tip, naming the practices it addresses centrally.

The First Months Launch List

Preparing

Usually it makes sense to undertake a light prep for LLtM during the last months of an academic year, leading up to a full launch around the beginning of the next academic year. Here are some important elements of this prep. You might undertake these solo or in conversation with a few others.

☐ *Review* three or four examples of the LLtM pictures of practice. Think about the general commitments and aspirations of your school. Very broadly, what might LLtM in your school look like? Make a short list of what seem like important features. (Practices: shared vision)

☐ *Consider* your timing: Is now the right time to embark on LLtM or is there something else to finish first? Or can what's already underway be woven in? Beware of too many moving parts at one time. Reduce them or envision how they can fit together. (Practices: shared vision)

☐ *List* three or four established or developing initiatives in your school (core commitments, courses, programs, etc.) that seem strong and that reflect LLtM as you imagine it for your school. How do these align with some of the Beyonds? How are they like the LLtM pictures of practice you read? What might it look like to push these initiatives forward? (Practices: shared vision)

☐ *Speculate* without commitment on an area or two not on the list above that might add a new spin to learning that matters in your setting—perhaps something that's "in the air" or that you've been wondering about. How do these areas match up with the general direction and commitments of the school and the Beyonds? (Practices: shared vision)

☐ *Craft* a school theme or vision in the form of a short paragraph for the learning that matters in your school. What is the learning that will matter most for the families and communities your school serves? How is this connected to the Beyonds? The vision can be—in fact should be—roomy rather than strict, allowing various points of entry. For instance, look back to the paragraph on page 53 about the Penbank focus on investigation, inquiry, and learning to learn, or at other examples in Part I, Pictures of Practice. (Practices: shared vision)

☐ *Share* the basic idea of LLtM with key staff members and the board early in the process. Seek affirmation from key faculty members and the school board that the school will seriously engage LLtM, at least to see how it goes. (Practices: shared vision, collaborative structures)

☐ *Explore* possible first steps with a few people who might play key roles in the initiative, if you haven't already. Who might be important people to involve? Who are the vital voices to engage to create a vision of the learning that matters? What beginning steps should be taken and in what direction? (Practices: collaborative structures)

☐ *Announce* the initiative to the general staff and other important stakeholders as "something coming" for the new academic year. Share why this is important and frame the initiative as collaborative and visionary, something to be collectively constructed by the school with great flexibility for patterns of participation. Or if you prefer, this can be announced at the beginning of the new academic year. (Practices: shared vision).

Launching

As a broad generalization, the best time for LLtM to establish serious momentum is around the beginning of an academic year, before everything settles into its usual pattern (with some prep during the previous year, as discussed earlier). Of course, if a different moment seems likely to work for your setting, by all means, take advantage of it!

☐ *Introduce* the initiative in more detail to the general staff and any other important stakeholders near the beginning of the new academic year. Remind everyone of the importance and the flexibility. Emphasize that the beginning period will be reflective and exploratory, focusing on constructing a broad vision. No one is being asked to make changes in anything immediately. Announce a few exploratory first steps. (Practices: shared vision, collaborative structures)

☐ *Share* some illustrative ideas about how other schools have interpreted learning that matters to clarify the concept, but emphasize that your school will build its own vision. This can be supported by an online or PDF version of the framework and/or examples, or examples you find elsewhere in the spirit of learning that matters. (Practices: shared vision)

☐ *Map* promising steps in more detail for the first few months of the academic year, in collaboration with your colleagues. How should expectations be established? What are some ways to build momentum for the initiative? (Practices: collaborative structures)

☐ *Develop* in particular a process with leader figures for building the school's conception of learning that matters. Involve representatives of different disciplines. Participants review what the school does well and what it most wants to hold onto, its abiding commitments, its identity. (Practices: collaborative structures)

☐ *Establish* ways to have ongoing, shared, and documented conversations about ideas toward learning that matters; for instance, develop broad categories populated with sticky notes. Find ways to involve the board and perhaps some parents and students. Look back at the example on page 54 of the staff process using stickies in the staff room from Good Shepherd, or other examples in Part I, Pictures of Practice. (Practices: collaborative structures)

☐ *Encourage* regular discussion of LLtM and the emerging conception of learning that matters for your institution during general and disciplinary staff meetings. Consider breaking down silos through some groups that meet across divisions and roles. (Practices: shared vision, collaborative structures)

☐ *Establish* through a participative process some broad tentative headlines for the school's principal themes toward learning that matters. Share emerging views for critique and further suggestions from all. (Practices: shared vision, collaborative structures)

☐ *Foster* an open and evolving vision going forward. The vision should be open enough to allow for diverse initiatives within it. Also, there's no need to carve the vision in stone. It can undergo tweaks and larger adjustments. (Practices: shared vision)

Deepening

As a vision begins to emerge after the very first months, reach out to faculty members to find out about ongoing programs and initiatives, and possible new initiatives from staff, that are aligned with the vision. Encourage and begin to document action on the ground. It's fine to start small.

☐ *Seek* staff members who are already teaching in ways well-aligned with the emerging vision. Encourage them to continue, sharpening and documenting their practice. (Practices: individual development)

☐ *Encourage* staff members to begin to draw out implications for which ideas, themes, or topics to bring more into the foreground in their teaching/learning. Seek champions who will set innovative directions, explore teaching approaches, tweak courses, or design new courses in the direction of the emerging vision. For instance, look back to the example from Beaconhills College on page 54, where champions innovated within what they were already doing, or other examples from Part I, Pictures of Practice. Remember that champions sometimes emerge from the places you'd least expect. (Practices: individual development)

☐ *Introduce* opportunities for professional development aligned with available resources and individual and department initiatives. Needs here can range from hardly any to significant, depending on prior experience of staff members and how far proposed innovations step beyond current practice. (Practices: individual development, sustained progress)

☐ *Maintain* communication with and involvement of the board and parents as LLtM moves forward. Both board and parental input and commitment are important. For instance, look back at the program of parent involvement from Westbourne Grammar School mentioned on page 55, as well as other examples from Part I, Pictures of Practice. (Practices: shared vision, collaborative structures, sustained progress)

☐ *Make room* for those who are cautious or skeptical but who can be helpful. Encourage them to be part of the conversation. If they are worried about X, what are their or others' ideas about how X might be addressed? Be cautious about pressuring those who are, at this point, not at all interested. Welcome minor participation. Avoid polarizing the staff into an in-group and the resisters. (Practices: collaborative structures, individual development)

☐ *Engage* collaboratively the question, "What, generally speaking, are we not going to do or going to do less of?" Some new directions emerging from the vision may pose challenges of finding classroom time and/or teacher collaboration time. There are many creative ways of addressing this through synthesis or compromise, generally without sweeping policies. The question of what not to do is best engaged around this point, after a positive vision has begun to emerge. (Practices: shared vision, sustained progress)

☐ *Establish* a regular pattern of communication and ways of reporting back on the advance of ideas and on practical experiments. Sustain a sense of a process in motion. As you go forward, you'll want to adjust toward what people experience as a productive but not disruptive pace. (Practices: collaborative structures, sustained progress)

On the Journey Together

You have to be able to bounce ideas off good ideas, to be able to challenge yourself and your thinking with peers who are as invested in thinking about what's next as you are. The best part [of being in a cohort] is the collegial development of good ideas; good ideas become much better with good people weighing in, and it's been amazing to be with people who share the same singular and important focus on wanting to improve student learning. — *Tony Sheumack, Headmaster*

The LLtM journey can be a challenging one, requiring energy and perspective-taking that may be hard to find in the flow of leaders' already busy lives. Principals who have taken this journey have learned that, when possible, traveling *together* is better than going it alone. Inspiration, ideas, and support can often be found when leaders take this journey with others. They can give you encouragement when you are struggling, offer feedback when you are uncertain, and push your thinking when you need it most. This section offers some broad tips on how to do this with other leaders. It shares the wisdom from principals who have been on the LLtM journey and offers some suggestions about how you can create a model of support.

Convene a critical cohort

Before going too far, look across your landscape and find leaders from other schools who have an interest in LLtM. You might first find colleagues with whom you are familiar or who are working in similar contexts. That's a fine place to start, but bear in mind that on this journey, diversity is a powerful driver of learning. Look for a few leaders who are working in different kinds of communities from yours. They may hold interestingly contrasting visions of LLtM for their contexts. For example, in a recent LLtM cohort, the principals didn't all agree on a common program for their individual schools. Each school had its own situation, but they still served one another well as critical friends. Differences can help you (and your colleagues) sharpen the logic of your vision.

Make sure that the group of leaders is not too small. A small group might lose momentum if a few people need to miss a meeting or be away for various reasons. On the flip side, beware of convening too large a group. Too many leaders who aren't familiar with one another might not be able to easily create the close relationships and accountability you'll likely need. One LLtM cohort we worked with began with eleven school leaders, which was a good critical mass. If your group starts off smaller, keep an eye out for other leaders you might bring onto the journey.

Finally, be sure to have someone who can convene and facilitate to help steer the conversation in meetings and over time. This could be a member of the group or someone outside the group who is committed to supporting the group on its journey.

Make time and space sacred

The LLtM journey requires time and space. Groups who travel together find and protect moments to meet in order to share visions, discuss possibilities, and reflect on progress. Create a regular rhythm of gathering. It could begin as once a month. Then, after a few gatherings, the group reassesses if it needs to meet more or less often. Whatever the schedule, establish the norm that this time together is sacred and to be protected. The gatherings are places for deep thinking and listening, so be sure they aren't times when the leaders will be predictably tired or feel rushed.

In addition to *when* the group meets, *where* is also important to consider. One way to do this is to identify a place outside the workplace where leaders can't be easily interrupted. The gathering place is ideally one that invites members to unplug, reflect, and have provocative conversations. Think of a museum, a nature preserve, someone's home, or a library. If that is not possible or convenient, make sure to protect the time for the gathering and find a room or a setting that easily allows for the type of exploratory thinking and dialogue you'll need on your journey. Look for settings with comfortable chairs, spaces to scrawl on such as whiteboards, and places that allow for walks or exploration during breaks.

For example, one LLtM cohort created a rhythm of meeting for a full day every six to eight weeks. They rotated the location between a rural inn and an urban hotel. Both locations had meeting rooms equipped with note pads and whiteboards, and had quiet areas for reflection and outdoor spaces for members to take walks during breaks. Participants ate, laughed, and explored together outside of their discussions. One thing to keep in mind is that museums, libraries, and other public centers might have free spaces to offer. In sum, pay close attention to finding a *when* and *where* that best support the group process.

Step out, invite in

Two good ways to create strong bonds in your group are to find moments to visit provocative places and invite outside voices into the conversations.

Brainstorm with your colleagues about places that are doing interesting work on learning or leadership. Visiting such places creates moments for you and your group to "step out" of your contexts. These could be visits to a nearby hospital, an innovative business, or a technology group that is exploring themes related to LLtM. These experiences of seeing how other organizations lead learning that matters in interesting ways stimulate thinking about one's own context. Visiting places together creates shared experiences that can also help the group grow closer.

In addition to visiting interesting places, identify experts you can invite into some of the gatherings. These could be academics, leaders, writers, or others who are exploring ideas related to learning and leadership. Perhaps they have written something that the group can read in advance. Such guests can present or share ideas with the group and engage the group in discussing how their ideas translate into the cohort's contexts. Such visits to sites or invitations for guests to share at gatherings provide valuable outside voices that can help stimulate new thinking and create shared experiences for your cohort.

Share and challenge

Creating a sense of trust and commitment to one another's development in the cohort is important for your journey. Set up norms that support confidentiality, close listening, and psychological safety so that it feels all right to challenge one another's thinking.

Design group rituals or routines that can build open and trusting relationships among participants. For example, at the beginning of their journey together, one LLtM cohort encouraged individuals to speak about their dreams and worries in their contexts. As one LLtM principal noted, while each leader was working on different initiatives, the group worked best when they remembered that "no one had the answers. . . . We argued without conflict and we asked questions to push one another's thinking."

Creating norms and opportunities for members to ask for help, share concerns, and disclose uncertainty allows for the vulnerability needed to build trust in the group. Facilitators can often help design and move groups into these sorts of sharing and challenging conversations. For your gatherings, it might mean creating moments for paired or smaller group discussions with clear prompts. It might mean creating norms for time limits or structuring discussions so everyone can participate.

As your group moves through the LLtM journey, remember that thinking and practices will and

should change. That can be a difficult and vulnerable space for many leaders. As another LLtM leader noted, "It requires that we share personal experiences, let go of our egos, so that the group can be a safe and open place to be curious with each other."

Document to see progress

Finally, be sure to chart the journey through an ongoing process of documentation (see the Documenting Learning that Matters tool in Part III). Documentation in the group is how the members observe, record, interpret, and share the process and products of their learning through a variety of media. It could mean gathering written reflections or photographs that the group revisits over time to see how members' thinking is evolving. Perhaps leaders bring in video-recorded interviews with stakeholders about learning that matters and a discussion ensues. Artifacts, whether from the group or brought in by individual members, can anchor conversations about LLtM. For example, one LLtM cohort developed a practice of beginning their meetings by sharing documentation of what learning that matters looks like in their contexts. These were examples of student work, photographs, student interviews, and other types of evidence that the group could observe and interpret.

You could also consider inviting the group to journal and revisit their entries to discuss how their thinking is developing over time. Distilling what the group is learning into brief documents after each meeting is another form of documentation that the group could revisit in the next meeting. Having members bring in documentation of student learning and engage in documenting their own learning will enable the group to focus their discussions and track progress.

Defining the learning that matters and leading change in your school can be a challenging journey. A small group of critical friends to support your thinking can make a big difference. They can pick you up, spark new ideas, and be thoughtful sounding boards for ideas. Learning with and from others—whether they be leaders from a very different school or thinkers from a different industry—can provide the stimulation and guidance you may need on your journey.

The advice in this section hopefully gives you some lessons learned from leaders who have gone before you. In the next part of the book, you will find a variety of tools that may also serve you well on the road ahead.

Part III
Tools & Tips

Building and Refining Visions for Learning that Matters

The heartbeat of Leading Learning that Matters is the quest for learning that truly matters in the lives learners live. As discussed earlier, "learning that matters" means learning likely to come up later with some frequency in significant ways; learning that helps students to understand the world around them and informs and inspires their actions; and learning grounded in the history, commitments, and aspirations of the institution in question.

The goal is certainly not just "mattering" in some ultra-practical and concrete sense. We want learners with insight into everyday scientific or historical perspectives that matter in their lives. We want students with social responsibility, good human relations, productive job performance, aesthetic engagement, and more.

As discussed in the section *Visions of the Learning that Matters*, the challenge of learning that matters emerges from educational business-as-usual. Traditional curricula are replete with themes and topics that have some technical or informational significance in the moment and reflect a traditional canon of learning, but that are not likely to matter very much to most learners' lives in the long term, especially beyond school itself.

Of course, learning that matters to most students in an ongoing way isn't everything. Students with a particular passion or need for a topic should have the chance to pursue it. Also, students need opportunities to discover their passions. Sometimes practicalities of national standards, mandates, and college admission expectations rule the situation. All that acknowledged, the complexity of the contemporary world, challenges of student motivation, and the richness of the lives that students have an opportunity to live recommend reconsidering what we teach and upping attention to learning likely to be meaningful in an ongoing way.

So to the practical question: *How to find such themes and topics?* The section *Visions of the Learning that Matters* explored this question in a general way. Bundled here are some simple strategies to support the process. The idea is to apply these tools in an institutionally-appropriate way to develop a vision of learning that matters, as well as particular themes and topics.

Finding Candidate Themes and Topics for Learning that Matters

The first group of tools concerns not finalizing general directions or topics or themes, but generating good candidates.

Beyonding Education. This invites educators to rethink current content toward learning that matters using six themes, including 21st century skills, global perspectives, interdisciplinary understandings, and more.

Mattermatics. This simple and playful brainstorming tool invites educators to think of one topic they don't now teach that they might add (+1), one topic they do now teach that they might expand (x2), and one topic they teach that they might shrink to make room (÷3).

Expanding Topics to Matter More. This tool offers several ideas for taking a currently taught topic and expanding it toward more learning that matters.

Evaluating a Theme or Topic for Learning that Matters

The two tools in this second group offer ways of checking whether a candidate theme or topic is really likely to pay off in the long term for learners.

Opportunity Story. This invites us to tell a story to ourselves about how a candidate theme or topic might deliver value in the long term.

Accept No Substitutes. This tool offers a checklist of important criteria for good learning—such as deep learning and rigor—that we want to honor, but that don't necessarily go as far as learning that matters. Experience shows that sometimes these are taken as substitutes for learning that matters. We want these characteristics and even more!

In both groups, each tool offers a Question & Answer component with basic tips about how the tool works.

Speaking of Question & Answer, this question arises: *Which tools to use?* Answer: Whatever is helpful! Or make up your own tools. Or don't use any tools at all, winging it based on your personal sense of the matter. Just try to pay attention both to the creative side of learning that matters, generating some good candidates, and to the critical side, analyzing whether these candidates are really likely to deliver in the long term.

Tools for Crafting Vision and Topics

Q & A

Where did these "Beyonds" come from? We surveyed informally a number of school curricula and government frameworks and formulated the Beyonds to characterize the trends emerging around the world toward educational innovation.

The Six Beyonds seem to overlap some. Am I using the right one? They do overlap to an extent. For instance, taking a global perspective on a topic might make it more interdisciplinary also. That's a bonus, not a problem.

Should I rethink my whole curriculum with the Beyonds? In most cases, trying to do everything at once is disruptive. It usually makes sense to start with a few promising opportunities.

If you're planning a brand new course, you might want to try to infuse it with the Beyonds from the beginning, but usually we're revising or extending something we already teach.

How far should I go? This is a judgment call, a matter of how much time and energy and interest you have. But here's one tip: Don't let beyonding become merely a gesture to make, like having your students use a 21st century skill once a week. Excellent traditional learning always trumps mediocre beyonding.

Should my school eventually pursue all the Beyonds equally? Not typically, no. Trying to do everything can be confusing. In our experience, schools attempting this sort of innovation develop their own distinctive profiles. This is part of constructing the vision for the school.

When I see ways to beyond a theme or unit, should I put the new material at the end? Start introducing the new material early in the unit. Expansions of scope should be part of the learning process early on. Broader themes placed toward the end tend to drop off the end when things get busy.

Can I beyond any unit or theme? Not every unit or theme is equally responsive. Some technical areas traditionally deemed important in the disciplines may not stretch very well. You might want to keep them as they are. Or you might want to shrink them if you feel they don't serve students well overall, depending on your general situation.

Beyonding Education

Consider a content area and search for units and big themes "beyond" the usual range

Beyond Academic Engagement
Fostering personal significance, commitment, and passion
e.g., offer experiential learning in the local community; offer learner choice beyond the typical use of electives

Beyond Content
Developing 21st century skills and competences
e.g., integrate perspective-taking and decision-making into history or literature, scientific ways of reasoning into science

Beyond Local
Embracing global perspectives, problems, and studies
e.g., look at local and regional issues as they appear elsewhere in the world; address global problems; compare and contrast perspectives from different cultures

Beyond Topics
Transforming topics into tools of broad understanding
e.g., turn particular cases in history, art, science, etc. into lenses to compare and contrast with other related cases; explore applications far wider than usual; look at particular topics through umbrella themes

Beyond Traditional Disciplines
Renewing and extending the disciplines
e.g., offer courses on less familiar but powerful themes; foreground the contemporary; "learn backward" by starting with contemporary matters and looking back to their origins and comparisons

Beyond Discrete Disciplines
Embracing interdisciplinary topics and problems
e.g., address themes that invite interdisciplinary perspectives & approaches; examine issues for one discipline generated by another

Q & A

How does this go with Beyonding Education and the upcoming Expanding Topics? Mattermatics seems to offer considerably less specific guidance. Yes, that's the point! It's brainstormy, loose, intuitive. Sometimes that's just what might work best. And, of course, you can use Mattermatics *with* the others.

Mattermatics includes not only expanding but shrinking—the divide-by-3. How come? It's about time we faced that challenge. One can't keep expanding in some places without shrinking in others. In fact, let's focus here on topics to shrink, since we haven't discussed shrinking much.

Why does shrinking come last: +1, x2, ÷3? Because it's very hard to ask what you might shrink in order to make room for material you haven't even imagined yet. It's much easier to create a new vision of what you'd like to teach first, and *then* ask how to make room for it.

What does shrinking involve in practical terms? Shrinking a topic can mean many things: concentrate on the basics of the topic. Go over the content without attaching complicated assignments to it so students get "acquaintance knowledge," which can often serve well as far as it goes. Make the topic a sub-topic of a larger topic, the sub-topic treated more briefly (but often more meaningfully) in a larger context. Some topics you might simply drop.

There are some topics I almost have to teach for various reasons—what then? Teach them, of course, with as much energy and motivation as you can! The world of education and the world in general are complicated places, there are many goals to be served, and every minute of every day does not have to aspire to this concept of *learning that matters*.

What about topics that I don't have to teach but that I love and some students love, even if they're hard to revise into learning that matters in our sense? Teach them if you can find the bandwidth, or as part of elective courses, or as options for students to pursue in groups. Certainly part of our role as educators is to awaken students to what might be of special interest to them, even if it is not likely to pay off in the long term for most students.

Mattermatics

Pick a course or unit you teach and try this...

 What's one theme or topic you could add to what you teach, to nudge the content toward learning likely to matter more in the lives of your learners in the long term?

 What's one theme or topic you already teach that you could expand in directions likely to matter more?

 What's one theme or topic you already teach that you could shrink some because compared with others it does not seem likely to matter enough to the lives of your learners in the long term?

 **A simple way to get started on learning that matters**

Q & A

How is this different from Beyonding Education? In general, Beyonding Education is more about ways to add whole new units or themes. Expanding Topics is about ways to stretch specific topics or themes you already teach. Really, however, either can be used for the other purpose.

You'll notice that Beyonding Education and Expanding Topics touch on some of the same ideas in different ways. Go with what works for you or play with them both!

Why might I want to use Expanding Topics? Most teachers have topics they like to teach or have to teach, but would love to make more of, enriching them and connecting them more broadly with the lives learners live. Expanding Topics offers several ways to do that.

There are some topics I teach that students find very conceptually challenging—is that a good place to start? On the whole, it's better to start with topics that are substantive but not topics where students really struggle. Start from strength! After all, you are trying something new . . . why try it on a topic that's already especially difficult?

However, if students find a topic not so much conceptually challenging as dull, such a topic might be a good place to start, since expanding usually energizes a topic.

When I expand a topic, should I put the extensions at the end? Start on Day 1 or soon after. Expansions of a topic generally make it feel more relevant and energizing for students. Also, expansions placed toward the end often do not get the attention they deserve because things have gotten busy.

Can any topic be expanded? As with units and themes under Beyonding Education, not every topic is responsive. Some important technical topics in the disciplines do not stretch very well. You may want to keep them as they are. Or you may want to shrink them if you feel they don't serve students well overall, depending on the situation.

Expanding Topics to Matter More

How can I stretch this topic in the direction of more resonance with the lives learners are likely to live?

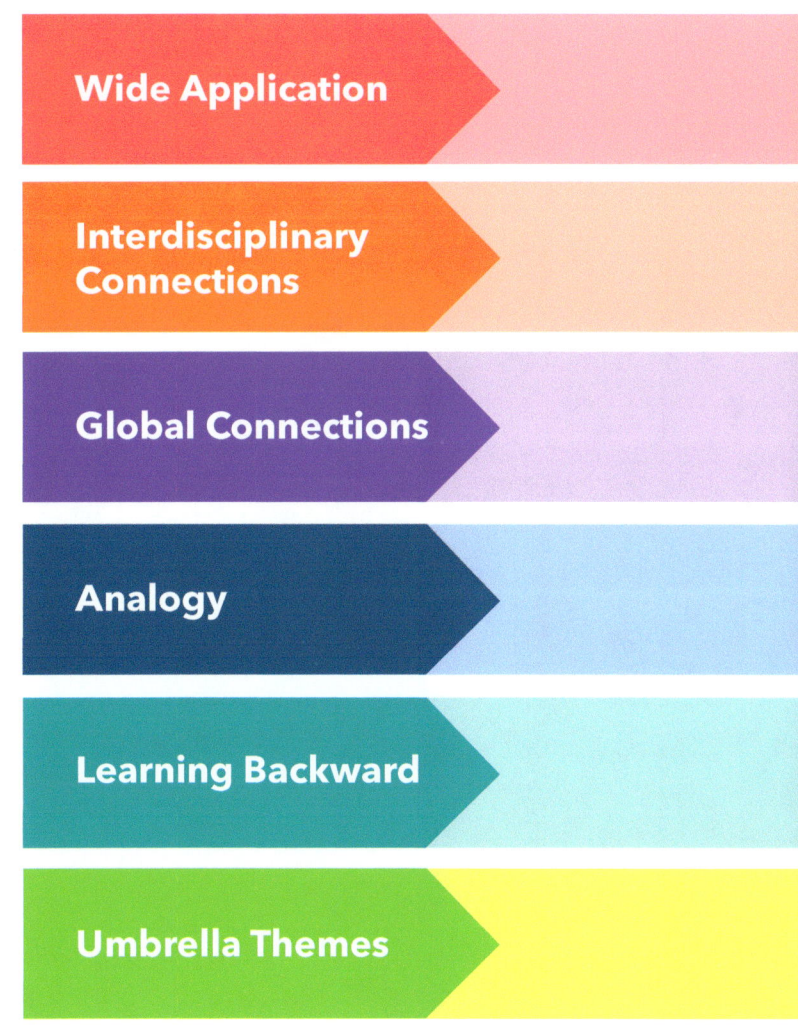

- Wide Application
- Interdisciplinary Connections
- Global Connections
- Analogy
- Learning Backward
- Umbrella Themes

| **Wide Application** | General theories and frameworks are in principle ready to matter more. Unfortunately, typical treatment of them settles for a narrow range of standard problems of application, the list of 10 or 15 problems or think-about-this questions at the end of the chapter. Reach further! |

| **Interdisciplinary Connections** | Connect a disciplinary topic to other themes in other disciplines by means of a cross-cutting topic, often in a world-scale problem. |

| **Global Connections** | In a complex world, reaching for global connections provides a natural way to amplify many topics. |

| **Analogy** | Episodes of history, works of literature, biological organisms, and many other particulars invite expansion by analogy: What are other cases with a somewhat similar character? At a deeper level, how are they the same, and how different? |

| **Learning Backward** | Usually we proceed historically, studying history or literature or even science in the order it developed. Suppose we start with now instead and then reach back. |

| **Umbrella Themes** | Frame the topic with broad themes that foster higher levels of understanding and connection-making far and wide. |

Expanding Topics to Matter More

Example — The typical approach to Newton's laws involves a few problems of standard types. Suppose the class examines two or three everyday phenomena strongly shaped by Newton's laws. Then the students undertake investigations of their own out-of-school environments, such as sports, to find Newton's laws at work in significant ways.

Example — Students studying economics might get a bigger picture through an interdisciplinary cross-topic like the world of oil: economics, politics, and ecology.

Example — Literature, stories, parables, or sagas in one's own culture can be compared with those from others. Or for ecology, how do problems like water shortages appear in different parts of the world? How are they perceived? How are they dealt with?

Example — In studying the French Revolution, one can go on to ask: How well do its dynamics match the Russian Revolution or the American Revolution? Or even the Industrial Revolution?

Example — Learn some physics "backward" by beginning with contemporary problems of energy. Learn some biology backward by beginning with contemporary problems of contagious diseases spread through international travel, or controversies around genetic engineering, or current waves of extinction. Learn some history backward by beginning with the Arab Spring and its complicated and still unfolding fate.

Example — Suppose that students are studying familiar elements of biology—cells, photosynthesis, food chains. Here are some umbrella themes that might give these important themes even more scope: energy flow and energy budgets, adaptation and adaptive trade-offs, social organisms and their very different societies.

Q & A

Who might tell opportunity stories? Teachers thinking about what they teach or could teach, and department heads and others thinking about the overall curriculum, with learning that matters in mind. Sometimes in conversation with others, exchanging perspectives.

Why is it helpful to tell opportunity stories for a theme or topic? Sometimes a theme or topic sounds good, sounds important . . . but would not actually surface that often or significantly in the lives most learners are likely to live. Trying to tell an opportunity story is a way of testing by calling upon our general sense of how the world works.

And there is a bonus: telling an opportunity story can help in planning teaching. It reveals some opportunities for future use to bear in mind as you teach!

What kinds of opportunities count? Many kinds—everyday practical contexts, questions of value, social and civic responsibility, human relations, collaboration, insights into the world one encounters even if one isn't deeply involved (e.g., major world events, big scientific discoveries), artistic experiences, etc.

With all those kinds of opportunities, couldn't we make some kind of a learning that matters case for just about any content? Not if we are honest with ourselves. To be sure, we can say X might happen or Y might happen, and, if it did, students might make connection A or B. However, we have to ask ourselves: How often? With what significance? How likely is it that students will even remember the content by then?

We have to ask ourselves: Are we just trying to make a case for something we've always felt is important rather than really considering the likely trajectories of students' lives now and later?

But how can we be sure what lives learners are likely to live? We cannot, of course. Education has always involved guesses about what students will need. It's no different here, except we are trying to make more informed guesses!

What if a theme or topic I like does not lead to a good opportunity story? What if it's hard to find what seem like good opportunities? Maybe you can stretch the theme or topic, frame it more broadly, combine it with another, etc. Or maybe in the end you will want to swap it for something a little different.

Or maybe in your context you will decide to teach it anyway, not as learning that matters broadly for students, but because students need it in a strictly academic sense or to awaken to the theme those students who might be particularly interested. There are many possibilities.

Opportunity Story

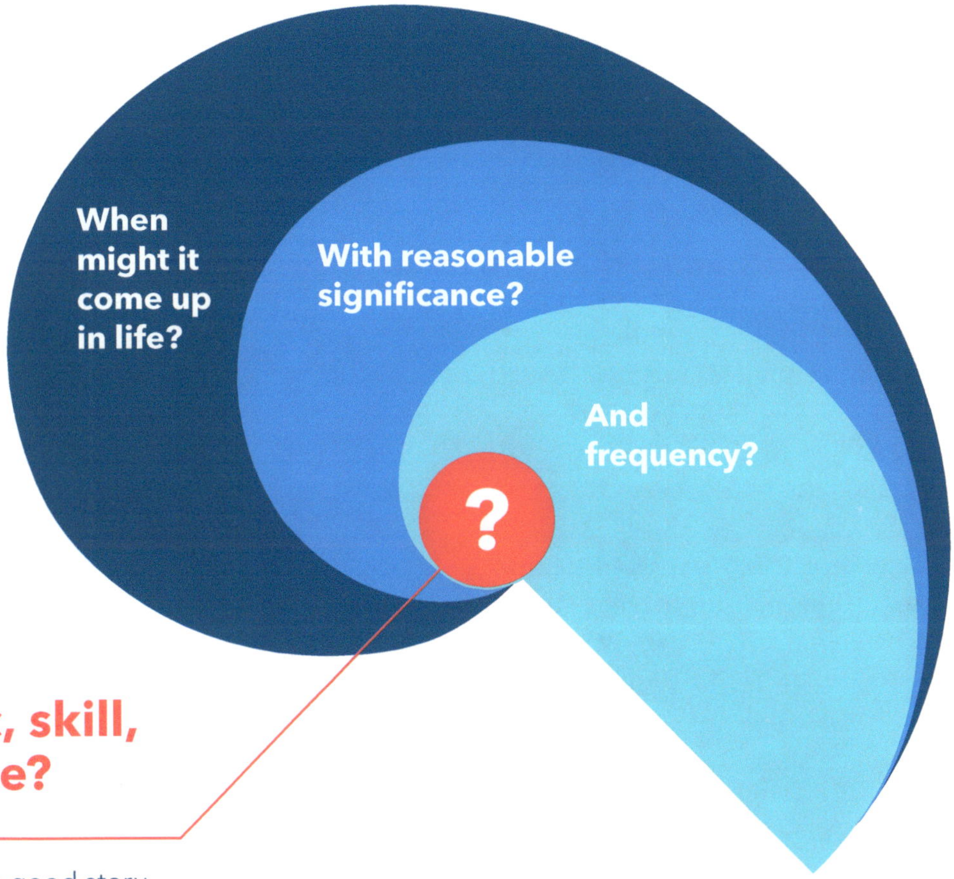

When might it come up in life?

With reasonable significance?

And frequency?

Topic, skill, theme?

Can I tell a good story for whatever lifeworthy theme or topic I have in mind?

If it's hard to find a convincing opportunity story, maybe I can stretch the theme or the topic or swap it for another.

Q & A

Why is the Accept No Substitutes checklist helpful? Participants in Leading Learning that Matters have found that it's all too easy to view academic criteria like deep learning or rigor as enough for learning that matters. But such criteria do not go far enough. The checklist is a tool for ensuring we have the difference in focus.

So criteria like deep learning or rigor are not important for learning that matters? They are important, of course! If students do not learn something with depth and reasonable rigor, it's not going to last in their minds and inform their lives.

What if a theme or topic I like does not seem promising for learning that matters? The answer here is the same as for Opportunity Story: Maybe you can stretch the theme or topic, frame it more broadly, combine it with another, etc. Or maybe in the end you will want to swap it for something a little different.

Or perhaps in your context you will decide to teach it anyway, not as learning that matters broadly for students, but because students need it in a strictly academic sense or to awaken to the richness of the theme those students who might be particularly interested.

Accept No Substitutes

There are many important qualities of learning that, in themselves, do not promise learning that matters in the long term. Test your idea for a theme or topic to be sure it offers more than these qualities. How many can you check off?

- ☐ **More than deep learning**
  We want deep learning but broad life relevance too.

- ☐ **More than understanding *of***
  We also want understanding *with*, e.g., learners would not only develop an understanding of basic probability but would use probability to understand many other things.

- ☐ **More than rigor**
  We want reasonable rigor, but rigor in itself does not make a topic or skill broadly worthwhile. Narrow topics or skills can easily be rigorous.

- ☐ **More than importance in the disciplines**
  We want topics important in their disciplines, but some topics have a mostly technical significance without speaking broadly to the lives learners will live.

- ☐ **More than the familiar disciplines**
  The familiar disciplines are rich sources of learning that matters. But so are some less often taught disciplines and interdisciplinary themes and skills.

- ☐ **More than practical topics and skills**
  We want these but not only these—much of learning that matters involves big ideas from art, science, or history that speak broadly to life and inform its value, without being "practical" in a narrow how-to-do-it sense.

- ☐ **More than transfer of learning within the discipline**
  We want transfer of learning, but transfer to what? Transfer of learning just to other technical contexts does not necessarily matter in the big picture. We want transfer to many life occasions.

- ☐ **Less than more, more, more**
  We want themes and units and topics that matter, but really, too much might reasonably matter. We cannot add it all, and we cannot keep everything we had before and add, add, add. We have to find ways to prioritize and shrink.

Leading Learning that Matters

The success of any change in a school is going to depend on how the leaders and the leadership team create the conditions for it to flourish. Moving a school toward the learning that matters invites leaders to consider how they can engage their staff, inspire students, and sustain the community's progress toward a vision of learning. It involves relationship building, listening, and negotiation. It involves staff development and creating a culture of collaboration. All these conditions and more have to be put in motion while balancing the political and economic demands of managing a school. While it is not easy and there is no magic recipe, the cases and ideas in this book illustrate the practices of many leaders who have navigated this path.

Leading Learning that Matters involves four overlapping core practices of leadership that are discussed in Part II of this book. *Creating shared vision* is the practice in which the leader becomes a change agent for the school by engaging others in crafting a guiding and evolving vision of the learning that matters. *Developing collaborative structures* is the practice of designing ways for teachers, students, and others in the community to listen, think, and experiment with one another. A shift to learning that matters may require teachers, parents, and students to learn new ideas and adopt new ways of learning. The practice of *supporting individual development* creates safe and stimulating conditions for others to develop their capacities. Finally, *sustaining progress* is the practice of embedding processes that support the learning that matters into the everyday work life of a school. These four practices are offered as a way to think about how to move forward over time.

How do leaders enact these practices? The earlier cases in this book illustrate and offer insights from the important variety of ways leaders have worked with their communities toward the learning that matters. A close read of those cases will show interesting differences and approaches. How leaders enact each practice depends on critical differences between their communities—the different values, strengths, and aspirations of their stakeholders. However, there are also some similarities across the cases. The tips offered in previous sections are a collection of strategies to keep in mind. In addition, it's important to remember that there are tools that can support those practices.

What follows are some concrete strategies that LLtM leaders have used in leading change initiatives. We hope that they will spark ideas about how you might adjust them to fit your specific context.

Documenting Learning that Matters. Borrowing from other Project Zero work, this tool offers leaders a way to gather and interpret evidence of what counts as learning that matters. It can be used across all four leadership practices.

Ecology of Social Influences. This is a tool to help you and others begin mapping out the variety of forces that are (and could be) shaping the learning that matters in your context. It can support thinking about how to develop collaborative structures and sustain progress.

Learning Frame & Windows. This tool assists leaders in naming the learning that matters and finding supportive examples. It can be used to develop shared vision and collaborative structures.

Voices to Vision. Creating shared vision enlists the perspectives of stakeholders about learning that matters. This tool offers guiding questions to involve students, parents, and faculty.

Ladder of Feedback. This tool provides a structure for offering critical and actionable feedback using four relatively simple steps: *clarify, value, puzzle,* and *suggest*.

Edge Effect. This tool helps leaders anticipate potential tensions that might surface as new elements for the learning that matters are introduced into the existing agenda of initiatives and projects. It invites leaders to create a synergistic edge between new ideas and established initiatives.

Key Change Roles. This tool invites leaders to map out the multiple roles that make up the ecology that the change will take place in, hence getting a good idea of the roles that are already filled and the ones that will need to be filled.

Tools for Leading the Process

Q & A

Why is it important to document the learning that matters? Creating examples of learning that matters enables leaders to communicate what it looks like to others and creates a collaborative structure for teachers to share their examples with one another.

What are some questions to keep in mind when sharing documentation? When sharing with students or colleagues, ask yourself: *Does the documentation focus on learning that matters, not just something we did? Does it promote conversation or deepen understanding about some aspect of learning that matters? Does it help me address a particular question I have about learning that matters in my school?* When sharing more broadly with others, ask yourself: *Does the documentation provide enough context for the viewer to understand the piece? Does it focus on learning that matters, not just on what was done? Does it focus on the process and the product of learning? Does it clearly communicate aspects of the learning that matters that I consider most important? Does it include interpretations by teachers and/or students? Does it promote conversation about learning that matters?*

Does the leader document or can the leader enlist others to do this? Both. Think about the kinds of evidence you see in your school that will help anchor discussions and model practices important for the LLtM process. Since you can't be in every classroom, enlist teachers to document. Be available so teachers can share evidence with you (and others) and involve you in interpreting the evidence.

What if I or my teachers don't have a lot of time to document? Documentation need not be time-consuming; large-scale documentation practices are built on smaller routines. Look for small ways to capture evidence already happening in the school and in classrooms—photos of community moments, pieces of student work, quotes overheard in meetings, etc. Carve out pockets of time to share and interpret these during staff meetings or other scheduled gatherings.

What are the skills needed to do this? A key skill is noticing, which might be difficult when people are busy! Noticing helps us to observe moments and also helps when we are sharing and interpreting. When sharing documentation, invite audiences to describe or recount what they see, not leap quickly to interpretations. Skills of noticing are a firm foundation on which to build documentation practices.

Documenting Learning that Matters
A tool for engaging the practice of documentation

- Curious noticing of surprising moments
- Intentional inquiry of moments with a question in mind

1 Observing
close looking for moments of learning that matters

- Individual reflection
- Sense-making with colleagues
- Engaging students in meaning-making

2 Recording
gathering evidence of learning that matters

3 Interpreting
making meaning of what learning that matters looks like

4 Sharing
engaging others in stories of what learning that matters looks like

- Images, voices, quotes, student work, video
- Capturing evocative moments that can be revisited
- Done by students, teachers, aides, parents, etc.

- Builds collective knowledge within and across classrooms
- Involves family and community members
- Sparks public exhibitions for a wider audience

Q & A

How do I begin the process of mapping the ecology of social influences in my setting? Use the following steps to guide your process:

Step 1: What is the learning that matters? In the middle of the tool, write down your current vision of learning that matters. This could be a revision of your school's current mission with a spin toward the Beyonds noted in the Visions of the Learning that Matters section.

Step 2: What and who are influencing the learning that matters? Locate how you see various stakeholders (students, parents, teacher teams, boards, etc.) or forces (state policies, assessments, school space, etc.) that might affect the learning that matters in positive and/or negative ways. Draw connections where natural among these stakeholders and forces.

Step 3: Share the map and revise it. Share your representation with some close colleagues and collect feedback. See what's missing and test your assumptions about the linkages.

Step 4: Consider next steps. Begin formulating a plan for ways to engage some key groups in the process. Consider how you will understand their needs, what roles you may ask them to play, and the ways you can involve them in experiments.

What if I'm not sure what to put in the middle as my vision of the learning that matters? Remember, this is an evolving document. So don't worry that what you initially write as your vision might not be permanent. It will more than likely change. If you feel stuck, review the Beyonding Education or the Mattermatics tools for some inspiration. Strive for some initial language that begins to depict the qualities of learning that matter most to you and your community.

What doesn't get listed as an influence? It's really up to you, but remember that when you share this with others, you invite them to react and be a partner in your thinking. Your initial list of stakeholders or forces should intentionally be broad—think of all the different sorts of people, policies, needs, values, initiatives, etc. that will play a part in the learning that matters.

Drawing lines between an influence and the vision feels too simplistic. Is there a better way to show the relationships? Play with your depiction; don't feel limited by the lines. It's just a starting point. Try using different colors, thicknesses, dotted lines, etc. to represent the more nuanced kinds of influences you see. Again, when you share this with others, getting feedback on how things relate is a place of focus. And likely there will be relationships between the stakeholders and forces, too. So try to find a way to show the complexity in order to spark conversation.

Ecology of Social Influences

A tool for articulating the variety of forces and stakeholders that may need to be involved in the learning that matters journey

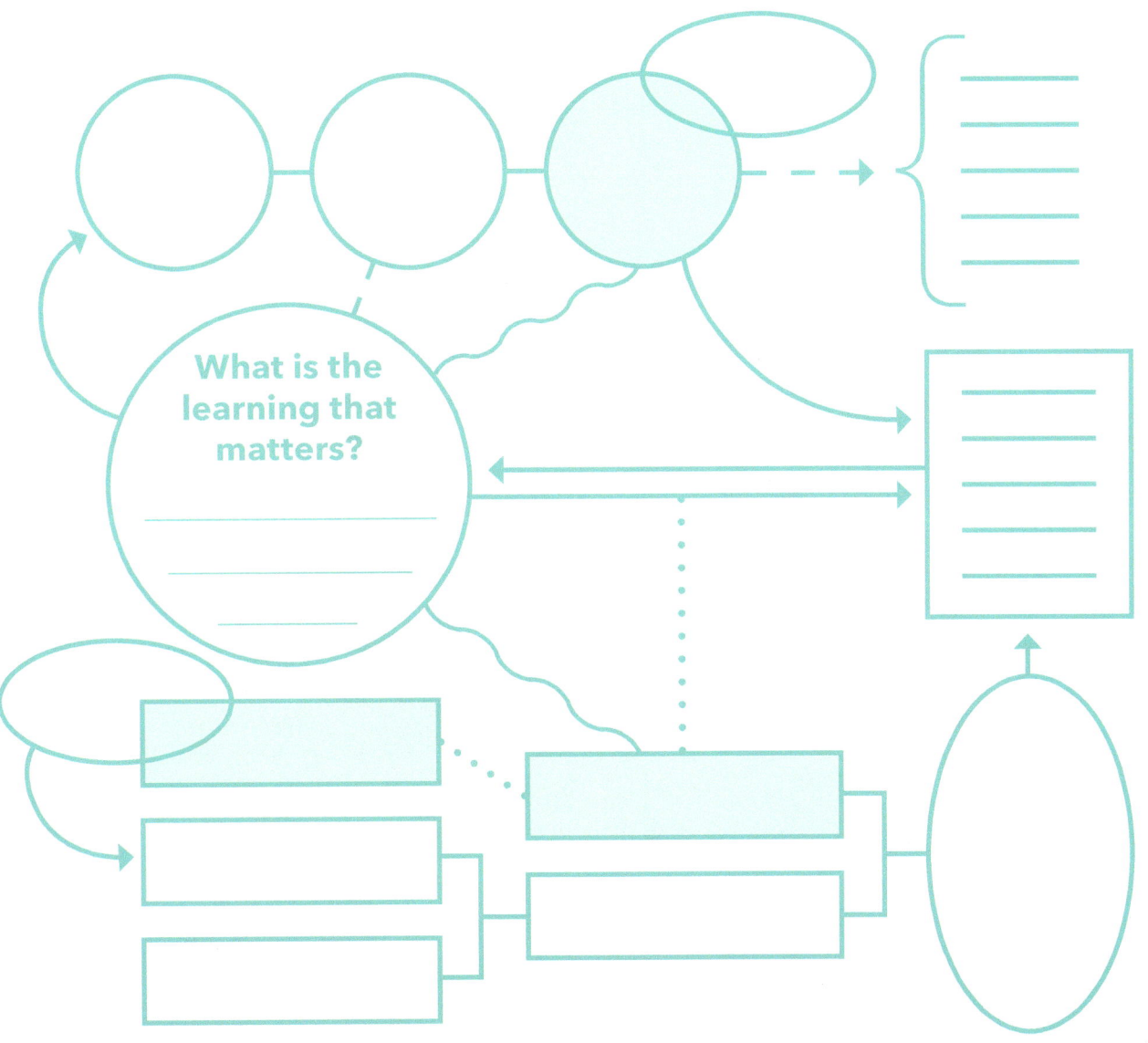

Q & A

What do frames, windows, and reflections refer to? Frames briefly articulate the learning that matters—why it is important and how it has been developed. Windows illustrate the learning that matters, for example, quick bullets or notes of examples that show the learning that matters and who is involved. Reflections briefly recap challenges, lessons, or other useful tips.

Should I begin with the frame or the windows? Either! It might feel helpful to articulate the frame first to hone what matters most. However, if there is some learning that matters already happening in your school that is iconic for the students and the community, start with that and ask, what is the learning that matters here? Existing windows can be interesting places from which to begin to craft frames.

Where does the frame come from? A vision of learning that matters comes from your and your community's sense of what is going to matter most for the lives your learners will lead. It could connect to elements of the school's current mission, but try to push beyond that. It could be your own sense of learning that matters that you test and refine through conversations with important stakeholders. Or it could originate from the stakeholders. What's important is that it is collaboratively developed and shared.

Can there be multiple frames? Strive for a single succinct statement that captures the essence of what matters most. While it's hard to leave things out, it is critical to exclude things that feel unfocused and uninspiring. If your vision has a few distinct ideas, play around with creating a frame and windows for each idea. Separating them might help you identify how they are similar and different.

Where do I find the windows? Look around; they might be in surprising places! Talk to students about the learning that matters to them and where it is happening. Talk to staff, family members, or other stakeholders who are attentive to the learning taking place. Ask questions that invite them to describe, in detail, what that learning looks like.

How many windows should I have? Collect as many as you can but decide which few you want to share more widely. Some windows may be better shared with different stakeholders. It's better to have a few illustrative and compelling examples to share. Avoid the temptation to share too many in a superficial way.

Learning Frame & Windows

A tool for describing the learning that matters and connecting it to examples of what it looks like in action

Frame How am I currently articulating the learning that matters for my school? Why is it important? Who has been involved in shaping it (teachers, students, families, school board, etc.)?

Windows What are 2–3 examples that illustrate what this learning looks like at my school (student work, a unit, exhibit, class project, etc.)? Who are the key players involved in these examples (students, teachers, parents, community members, etc.)?

Reflections What are 2–3 main surprises or challenges I've faced in leading this learning that matters? What are 2–3 insights, lessons, or tips I could offer to other principals who are interested in leading learning that matters in their schools?

Q & A

Where do I start? Anywhere! Consider starting with a group that has expressed interest or a need. Maybe your faculty has been discussing how to update the curriculum. Maybe parents have been feeling disengaged. Or perhaps students have been feeling that their voices are not included in school decisions as much as they should be. This can be a way for groups to be and feel involved in shaping the vision for the learning that matters.

How do I collect ideas? It's important to let people know why you're asking: you are genuinely interested in their ideas and are looking to gather a variety of perspectives towards a vision of learning that matters. You could create a survey, ask teachers or students directly, or have teachers and students interview each other (and the community) as part of the initiative. Plan to gather as much information as possible from as many stakeholders as you can, while understanding that you will likely not get everyone's voice into the mix. If you miss some voices, be sure to find ways to get their input as themes begin to emerge.

Can I ask other questions? Absolutely! The dots after the questions provided are an invitation for you to think of other ways to elicit ideas from your community about the learning that matters most to them. So, don't feel constrained by the tool's questions. Use them to create questions you think will work better for your community.

What do I do with all the ideas? Look for patterns. You might want to ask a small group to help, which could include teachers, students, or parents. As you comb through the various ideas, look for frequent words or examples. Look for categories of ideas or activities. Note things that do not seem to fit; not everything will. Play around with different ways to represent the vision that is emerging. Once you have a draft vision, test it with students, teachers, and your community to get their input. Not everyone will agree and not every idea will be represented, so be clear with people about this.

Voices to Vision

A tool for beginning to create a shared vision of the learning that matters

As you think about the life you want to lead...

- **Q** What are the most important knowledge and skills you want to learn?
- **Q** What has been the most important thing you're learning?
- **Q** _____

→ ? **Students**

As you think about the children and youth we are developing in our school...

- **Q** What are the skills and knowledge that are most important for them to understand to be productive citizens?
- **Q** What must they understand to be effective workers or leaders in society?
- **Q** _____

→ ? **Parents & Community**

As you think about the children and youth we are developing in our school...

- **Q** What are the skills and knowledge that are most important for them to understand to be productive citizens?
- **Q** What must they understand to be effective workers or leaders in society?
- **Q** _____

→ ? **Teachers & Staff**

Q & A

What should I keep in mind when working with the four steps? <u>Clarify:</u> The goal here is to gather information about ideas or points that are unclear, e.g., "Tell me more about…" or "When you mentioned X, what did you mean?" This ensures that everyone has a clear picture of the idea being presented before offering feedback. <u>Value:</u> Giving positive feedback is not about being nice; it's about being specific and concrete, e.g., "Because you included A and B, I can see how this idea is better than C." Highlight parts that feel strong and share your reasons. <u>Puzzle:</u> If you have real concerns about an idea, share them honestly and openly, e.g., "I'm puzzling about how this will be perceived by parents" or "I'm concerned about how this fits with A and B." The spirit here is putting frank worries on the table while exploring possible solutions. <u>Suggest:</u> Offer concrete and specific suggestions, e.g., "How about including X?"

How strictly should we follow the steps? Sticking with the steps is important. If the conversation jumps around too much, it can be very difficult for the person sharing an idea to track the different kinds of feedback. Also, starting with "Clarify" often ensures that everyone is clear before suggestions are offered. Go back to a step during the conversation if that feels natural. Following the steps strictly in early uses of the tool will set up clear norms and expectations.

What does the person who is sharing the idea do during this process? The person sharing the idea should remain silent after the "Clarify" step. Even if there's some back and forth, that person should not dominate the discussion. This tool is designed to invite effective feedback, not to help the person present an idea.

What if I sneak in suggestions early? Often, we find ourselves unwittingly offering suggestions as clarifications, e.g., "Have you considered trying X?" Using the ladder effectively requires discipline. Take time to learn how to ask genuine questions of clarification. If you hear yourself or others suggesting too early, name it and ask the person to hold on to that idea for later.

Should we document the conversation? Yes! Feedback is vital to the change and learning process. Ask the person sharing to take notes on what they are hearing, or have everyone jot down ideas in the "Notes" section that are then collected, or have someone scribe on a whiteboard during the discussion.

Ladder of Feedback

A tool for offering effective and actionable feedback

Notes

4 Suggest
What concrete next steps or actions could be considered?

3 Puzzle
What concerns do you have that could be further explored?

2 Value
Specifically, what do you really like, find strong and/or positive?

1 Clarify
What is unclear? What information do you need in order to know more about what is being shared?

Q & A

Where does the concept of an edge effect come from? The edge effect is an ecological concept that refers to the overlap where two different habitats (e.g., forest and field) meet. Species from both habitats grow in the overlapping edge, but sometimes the interaction of the species offers opportunities for emergence, and new species that have adapted to the conditions of the edge thrive. The edge becomes a space of constructive friction where the whole is greater than the sum of its parts.

How do edge effects apply to the LLtM change initiative? The concept spotlights generative tensions that invariably arise when schools adopt and nurture innovations while continuing to encourage worthwhile established initiatives. Use this tool to create synergies between what is new and what is already in play by identifying generative tensions between them. Figure out how to get the best of both new and familiar worlds.

How should I use this tool? In any system where something new is introduced, there's always an edge effect operating. Use this tool to map and leverage it. For instance, you may need to drop topics of study that are all-time favorites with teachers but that do not matter for the lives that students will live. That will make room for topics that reach toward the learning that matters. At the same time, identify how established topics that already reach for the learning that matters could be synergistic with the new elements, either by extending or stretching them in the direction of the learning that matters. Use tools like Accept No Substitutes, Opportunity Story, or Beyonding Education to figure out which topics to keep and which ones to drop.

Often when new initiatives are introduced, tensions arise between the broader purpose of the school and the preferred direction of individual departments or teachers. The tensions are real and valid. Turn them into generative tensions instead of letting them fester and become destructive. Ask: *How can we turn this problem into an opportunity?* For instance, excellent examination scores are not important in and of themselves but are the launchpad toward success in life. Ask teachers why excellent scores matter and their answers will likely align with the school's broader purpose of supporting learners to be successful in life. Clarifying what "success" looks like is a productive starting point for thinking about what and how innovations and the existing agenda can coexist to create a healthy edge.

Edge Effect

A tool for creating a synergistic edge between new ideas and established initiatives

1 Identify existing initiatives and projects that have been and continue to be worthwhile for your context.

3 Look for the new in the familiar and the familiar in the new

How are the new elements already in motion in existing initiatives and projects?

How might the new elements extend or enrich existing initiatives and projects?

How might existing initiatives and projects contribute to the new initiative?

2 Name the new elements introduced into your context as part of the LLtM initiative.

Q & A

What's the basic idea? Effective change in an organization almost always involves several different roles moving the initiative forward. Missing or ineffectively filled roles can easily lead to weak results. For instance, the executive support of the political visionary typically needs to be not only firm but conspicuous. People need to see from time to time that she/he is emphatically on board. Further, change initiatives do not run themselves; a practical visionary is needed to fulfill day-to-day functions. And change can falter simply because of a lack of resources—meeting time, key supplies, etc. For effective change, it is important to fill key roles.

Are there other roles? Sometimes. Feel free to add according to the situation and your context!

Are these roles formal positions? Not typically. They are more like areas of responsibility within larger positions. For instance, the executive of the organization functions as political visionary for the initiative, but that's a small part of his/her responsibilities. The practical visionary spends more time than the executive but usually has other responsibilities. Sometimes people change roles. Sometimes people play more than one role.

Who should use this tool? Typically, the political visionary, practical visionary, and planning group, if any, will use it to ensure that the roles are filled and operating well.

Why "partial participants"? Often, it's not smart or manageable for everyone to start an initiative as a "general participant" from the beginning. Some people are busy with other initiatives. Some are a little cautious. A community can polarize into two camps about an initiative and that can be very undermining. It is best to encourage people to be at least a little bit involved so that they know what's going on, rather than force immediate participation or require people to declare they are fully "in" or "out."

What about skeptics? There are always skeptics—sometimes loud skeptics, sometimes silent skeptics; sometimes with thoughtful reasons, sometimes more reflecting issues of turf and such. Skeptics should be treated respectfully because they can often offer thoughtful improvements. Even if not, one wants to avoid coercive moves that generate group polarization.

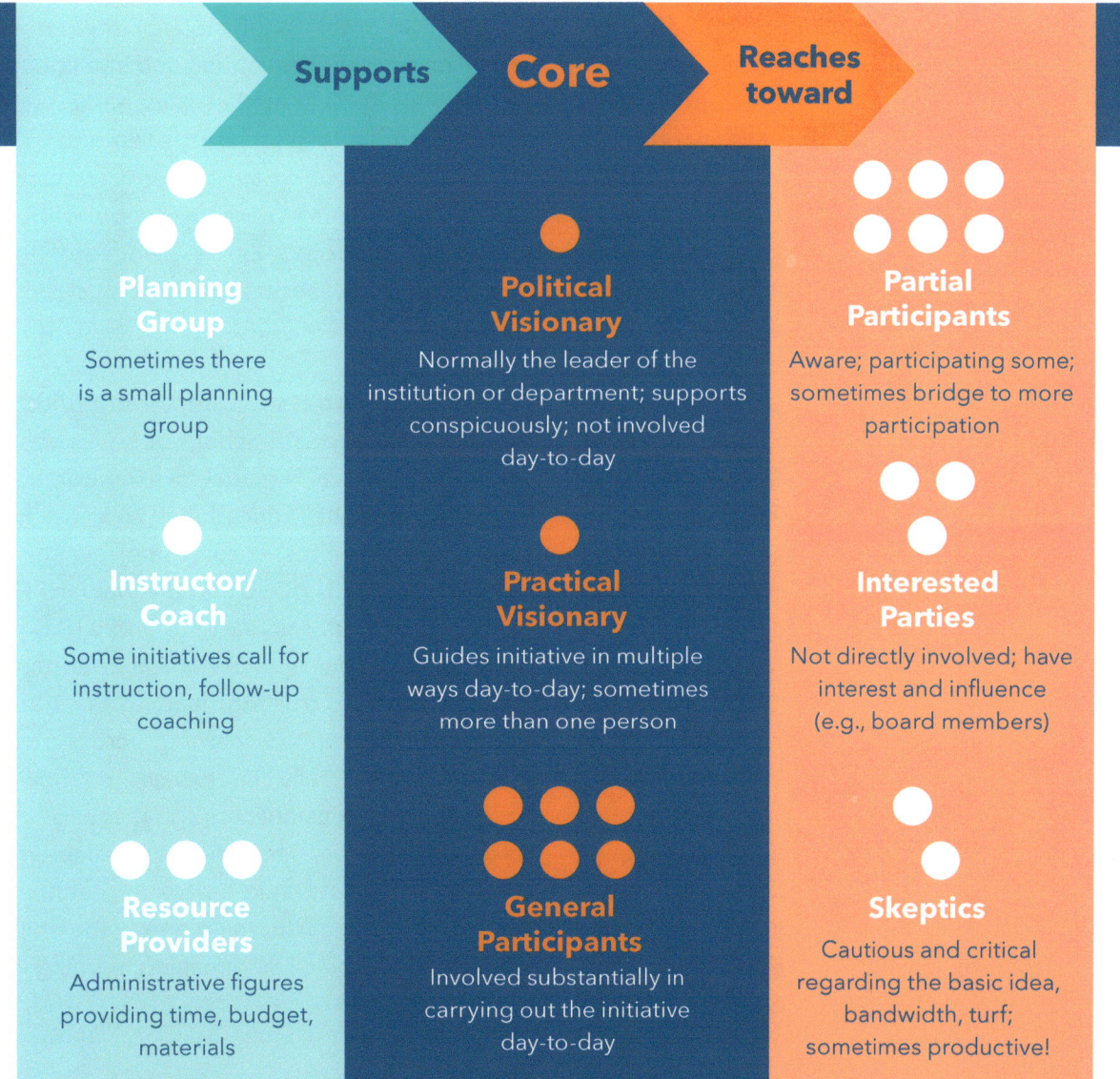

About the Authors

Flossie S. G. Chua is a Principal Investigator at Project Zero at the Harvard Graduate School of Education. Her work focuses on understanding how we can nurture good thinking and practices that develop the capacity for informed and positive action. Her projects explore emerging practices of progressive pedagogies in schools and the shared leadership structures that support them, and innovative paradigms for artists and the arts to operate in relationship to their communities and the world. Flossie also worked with ART21 Educators, a nonprofit designed to support K-12 teachers in bringing contemporary art, artists, and themes into classroom teaching and learning, and in broadening their curricular focus to include inquiry into contemporary issues and questions that demand cross-curricular knowledge and ways of thinking through contemporary art. She holds an Ed.D. from Harvard University and is an Instructor in Education at the Harvard Graduate School of Education.

David N. Perkins is the Carl H. Pforzheimer, Jr., Professor of Teaching and Learning, Emeritus, at the Harvard Graduate School of Education and a Principal Investigator at Project Zero. He conducts long-term programs of research and development in the areas of teaching and learning for understanding, creativity, problem-solving, and reasoning in the arts, sciences, and everyday life. He has also studied the role of educational technologies in teaching and learning, and has designed learning structures and strategies in organizations to facilitate personal and organizational understanding and intelligence. Dave received his Ph.D. in mathematics and artificial intelligence from the Massachusetts Institute of Technology and was a founding member of Harvard Project Zero at the Harvard Graduate School of Education. He served as Project Zero's co-director for nearly 30 years and now serves as senior co-director on its steering committee.

Daniel G. Wilson is the Director of Project Zero at the Harvard Graduate School of Education (HGSE), where he is also a Principal Investigator, a Lecturer at HGSE, and the Educational Chair at Harvard's "Learning Environments for Tomorrow" Institute—a collaboration with HGSE and the Harvard Graduate School of Design. His teaching and writing explore the inherent socio-psychological tensions—dilemmas of knowing, trusting, leading, and belonging—in adult collaborative learning across a variety of contexts. Specifically, he focuses on how groups navigate these tensions through language, routines, roles, and artifacts. This interest is reflected in three current focuses of Daniel's work: professional learning in communities, learning and leadership behaviors in the workplace, and making learning visible.

www.ingramcontent.com/pod-product-compliance
Lightning Source LLC
Chambersburg PA
CBHW042011150426
43195CB00003B/92